Life of Significant Soil

Celeste Foley
Freelance Monkette

ISBN: 1482515164
ISBN-13: 978-1482515169

DEDICATION

In 1995, I wrote an essay entitled "Gratitude" in which I thanked: "All the minds and muses who lived before and with me. Those who give me the books, poems, art, music, and voices which help deliver my soul to God. With their help, I travel through words, rhythms, visions, and ideas on my path. I am brought full circle from darkness to light, from misery to joy, from ignorance to understanding." This book based on my website is an homage to those minds and muses. I hope you enjoy, appreciate, and benefit from the deep humanity offered on these pages.

TABLE OF CONTENTS

ACKNOWLEDGMENTS

In his journal from July 1836, Ralph Waldo Emerson challenged:

"Make your own Bible. Select and collect all the words and sentences that in your reading have been like the blast of triumph out of Shakespeare, Seneca, Moses, John and Paul."

This I have done and so Life of Significant Soil was born.

PREFACE

"O God, by whose laws the poles revolve, the stars follow their courses, the sun rules the day and the moon presides over the night; and all the world maintains, as far as this world of sense allows, the wondrous stability of things by means of the orders and recurrences of seasons: through the days by the changing of light and darkness, through the months by the moon's progressions and declines, through the years by the successions of Spring, Summer, Autumn, and Winter, through the cycles by the completion of the sun's course, through the great eras of time by the return of the stars to their starting points." ~ St. Augustine

Nature provides us with a cycle of seasons which reflect the changing concerns of our lives. Winter is associated with depth and darkness so December is a time for God, January invites us into the dark night of the soul, and February delves into depression. Spring is associated with renewal so March transforms darkness to light, April emerges with new life, and May uses that new life creatively. Summer is associated with heat so June burns with passion, July smolders with romantic love, and August vibes with harmony. Fall is associated with harvest so September is concerned with ethical living, October ripens with wisdom, and November gives pause for reflection.

This book is www.lifeofsignificantsoil.com brought to paper. Please follow the calendar daily to keep pace with the flow of Life or use its wisdom and inspiration to support the seasons of your personal life.

JANUARY: DARK NIGHT OF THE SOUL

January 1ˢᵗ *Help Me Out God - Superchic*
"Mine, O thou Lord of life,
Send my roots rain."
~ Gerald Manley Hopkins,
"Thou Art Indeed Just, Lord"

January 2ⁿᵈ *The Great Beyond – REM*
"When I heard the learn'd astronomer, / When the
proofs, the figures were ranged in columns before me, /
When I was shown the charts and diagrams, to add,
divide, and measure them, / When I sitting heard the
astronomer where he lectured with much applause in
the lecture room, / How soon unaccountable I became
tired and sick, / Till rising and gliding out, I wandered
off by myself / In the mystical moist night-air, and from
time to time, / Look'd up in perfect silence at the stars."
~ Walt Whitman
"When I Heard the Learn'd Astronomer"

January 3ʳᵈ *Losing My Religion - REM*
"One by one, like leaves from a tree,
All my faiths have forsaken me."
~ Sara Teasdale, "Leaves"

January 4ᵗʰ *If There Is A God – The Smashing Pumpkins*
"It is not now as it hath been of yore –
Turn wheresoe'er I may, / By night or day,
The things which I have seen I now can see no more."

2

~ William Wordsworth
"Ode of Intimations of Immortality"

January 5th *Lord Is It Mine - Supertramp*
"You believe that one day you will walk out of this fog which surrounds you! Advance, advance; rejoice in death which will give you not what you hope for but a night still more profound, the night of nothingness.....My smile is a great mantle, which covers a multitude of sufferings. The sisters and people think that my faith, my hope and my love are profoundly fulfilling me, and that intimacy with God and union with His will, live in my heart. If they only knew...only blind faith moves me along, because the truth is that all is darkness for me."
~ St. Therese of Lisieux, *Last Conversations*

January 6th *Wooh God – Blind Melon*
"For when you first begin to undertake it, all that you find is a darkness, a sort of cloud of unknowing; you cannot tell what it is, except that you experience in your will a simple reaching out to God [a naked intent unto God]. This darkness and cloud is always between you and your God, no matter what you do, and it prevents you from seeing him clearly by the light of understanding in your reason, and from experiencing him in sweetness of love in your affection. So set yourself to rest in this darkness as long as you can, always crying out after him whom you love. For if you are to experience him or to see him at all, insofar as it is

possible here, it must always be in this cloud and in this darkness."

~ Anonymous 14th Century Mystic
The Cloud of Unknowing

January 7th *Troubles So Hard – Moby**
"O, life as futile, then as frail!
O for thy voice to sooth and bless!
What hope of answer or redress?
Behind the veil, behind the veil."

~ Alfred, Lord Tennyson , "In Memoriam AHH"
* I heard "troubles with," not "troubles but."

January 8th *God – Tori Amos*
"Finding is the first Act
The second, loss,
Third, Expedition for/the 'Golden Fleece'
Fourth, no Discovery –
Fifth, no Crew –
Finally, no Golden Fleece –
Jason – sham – too."

~ Emily Dickinson, "Finding is the First Act"

January 9th *Inside Out – Eve 6*
"Some have desired through hope to come to Thee,
And thou hast wrought in them their high design:
Lo! I have severed every thought from me,
And died to selfhood, that I might be Thine.
How long, my heart's Beloved? I am spent:
I can no more endure this banishment."

~ Abu 'l-Husayn al-Nuri
"I had supposed that, having passed away"

January 10th *Kum Ba Yah – Guadalcanal Diary*
"And malt does more than Milton can
To justify God's ways to man."
~ A.E. Housman, "A Shropshire Lad"

January 11th *Hey God – Bon Jovi*
"The experience of disenchantment is the beginning of mature religious consciousness... while the Sacred expresses itself through particular symbols, any simple identification of symbol and the Sacred is naive... In the Catholic world of the immediate past there was a tendency to merge the symbols of sacrality with the Sacred itself...Mystery had completely handed itself over to Church authority. In the process it ceased to be Mystery and became rule... Disenchantment is an experience of Mystery reasserting itself. Whenever a person mistakenly equates Mystery with finite reality, he creates an idol. An idol is not a symbol of Mystery but the pretension to be Mystery itself. It insinuates a total revelation and creates the false consciousness that Mystery has dissolved into total availability."
~ John Shea, *Stories of God*

January 12th *Terrible Lie - NIN*
"Turning and turning in the widening gyre
The falcon cannot hear the falconer."
~ W.B. Yeats, "The Second Coming"

January 13ᵗʰ *Dear God - XTC*
"O Thou, who in the heavens does dwell,
Who, as it pleases best Thysel',
Sends ane to heaven an' ten to hell,
A' for Thy glory,
And no for ony gude or ill
They've done afore Thee!
I bless and praise Thy matchless might,
When thousands Thou hast left in night,
That I am here afore Thy sight,
For gifts an' grace
A burning and a shining light
To a' this place."
　~ Robert Burns, "Holy Willie's Prayer"

January 14ᵗʰ *Shades of Grey – Billy Joel*
"May one, then, with due tentativeness and hesitation, speculate that for a comparativist, the truth may be conceptualized as something that is both immanent within, and transcends, any given formulation of it in any given system. So far as one's own system is concerned, where the immanence is most readily accessible, it is important, of course, to cling fast to that truth and at the same time in due humility to recognize as well the transcendence."
　~ Wilfred Cantrell Smith, *Faith & Belief*

January 15ᵗʰ *With God On Our Side – Bob Dylan*
"[The men who called for Socrates death] genuinely thought that Socrates was an atheist because his idea of

God had a philosophical depth that probed beyond traditional concepts. Not badness but blindness killed Socrates… intellectual and moral blindness is a dilemma which man inflicts upon himself by his tragic misuse of freedom and his failure to use his mind to its fullest capacity."
~ Martin Luther King, Jr., *Strength to Love*

January 16th *The Wanderer – U2*
"Freethinkers are those who are willing to use their minds without prejudice and without fearing to understand things that will clash with their own customs, privileges, or beliefs. This state of mind is not common, but it is essential for right thinking; where it is absent, discussion is apt to become less than useless."
~ Leo Tolstoy, *On Life and Essays on Religion*

January 17th *The Seeker – The Who*
"I repeated what I've said over and over again so many times in so many books: that homo religiosus thirsts for the real, that he wants to be, fully and at any cost."
~ Mircea Eliade, *Journals*

January 18th *Where Do I Go – Hair*
"All the great spiritual models of the ages before us found themselves, at one point or another, plunged into doubt, into darkness, into the certainty of uncertainty: Augustine, John of the Cross, Teresa of Avila, Meister Eckhart, John the Baptist, Thomas, Peter, one after another of them all wondered, and wavered, and

believed beyond belief. Doubt is what leaves us open to truth, wherever it is, however difficult it may be to accept... Without doubt, life would simply be a series of packaged assumptions, none of them tested, none of them sure, and all of them belonging not to us, but to someone else whose truth we have made our own."

~ Sister Joan Chittister, *Uncommon Gratitude*

**January 19*th* *Question – Moody Blues*
"Question with boldness even the existence of God; because if there be one, he must more approve of the homage of reason, than that of blindfolded fear."

~ Thomas Jefferson , *Letter to Peter Carr*, 8-10-1787

**January 20*th* *Is There Anybody Out There – Pink Floyd*
"Indeed, God always seems to us to be dead when we substitute our thoughts about him for living in response to him."

~ Reuel L. Howe, *The Miracle of Dialogue*

**January 21*st* *The First Time – U2*
"Friend, this is the only way
to learn the secret way:
Ignore the paths of others,
even the saints' steep trails.
Don't follow.
Don't journey at all.
Rip the veil from your face."

~ Sachal Sarmast

January 22nd Love Rescue Me – U2
"Love springs eternal!
When I learnt the lesson of Love
I dreaded going to the mosque.
Hesitantly, I found a temple
Where they beat a thousand drums.
Love springs eternal! Come!
I am tired of reading holy books,
Fed up with prostrations good.
God is not in Mathura or Mecca.
He who finds Him is enlightened!
Love springs eternal! Come!
Burn the prayer mat, break the beaker!
Quit the rosary, chuck the staff!
Lovers shout at the top of their voices:
Break all rules that tie you down!
Love springs eternal! Come!
Heer and Ranjha are united:
While she searches for him in orchards,
He is in her warm embrace!
She has her love, she is fulfilled!
Love springs eternal! Come!"
    ~ Abdullah Shah

January 23rd Where the Streets Have No Name – U2
"He dwells not only in temples and mosques –
The whole creation is his abode.
The whole world is bewitched by his tale,
but wise are those who are lost in his love."
    ~ Sarmad

January 24th *Still Haven't Found What I'm Looking For-U2*
"A true Lover doesn't follow any one religion, be sure of that. Since in the religion of Love, there is no irreverence or faith. When in Love, body, mind, heart and soul don't even exist. Become this, fall in Love, and you will not be separated again."
~ Rumi

January 25th *Carry On My Wayward Son - Kansas*
"Perplexed in faith, but pure in deeds,
At last he beat his music out.
There lives more faith in honest doubt,
Believe me, than in half the creeds."
~ Alfred, Lord Tennyson, "In Memoriam A.H.H."

January 26th *Testimony – Robbie Robertson*
"The relationship between commitment and doubt is by no means an antagonistic one. Commitment is healthiest when it is not without doubt, but in spite of doubt. To believe fully and at the same time to have doubts is not at all a contradiction: it presupposes a greater respect for truth, an awareness that truth always goes beyond anything that can be said or done at any given moment. To every thesis there is an antithesis, and to this there is a synthesis. Truth is thus a never-dying process."
~ Rollo May, *The Courage to Create*

January 27th *I Still Believe – The Call*
"You call for faith:

I show you doubt, to prove that faith exists.
The more of doubt, the stronger faith, I say,
If faith overcomes doubt."
~ Robert Browning, "Bishop Blougram's Apology"

January 28ᵗʰ *River Of Dreams – Billy Joel*
"Dust as we are, the immortal spirit grows
Like harmony in music; there is a dark
Inscrutable workmanship that reconciles
Discordant elements, makes them cling together
In one society. How strange that all
The terrors, pains, and early miseries,
Regrets, vexations, lassitudes interfused
Within my mind, should e'er have borne a part,
And that a needful part, in making up
The calm existence that is mine when I
Am worthy of myself! Praise to the end!"
~ William Wordsworth, "The Prelude"

January 29ᵗʰ *God-Shaped Hole - Plumb*
"Because truth is founded on that which is within us
and yet does not depend on us, on that which is the
most intimate aspect of our subjectivity and yet
common to the entire community of subjects, truth-in-
us depends on the existential attitude we freely adopt in
its regard...Every free human agent is necessarily faced
with the decision to accept or refuse the presence of
transcendence within his will. Depending on the
alternative chosen, the choice resolves itself either into
the existential identity of lived truth or the real

contradiction of lived error."
~ Ewert Cousins, *Conscience: Its Freedom and Limitations*

January 30th *Secure Yourself – Indigo Girls*
"The name of this infinite and inexhaustible depth and ground of all being is God. That depth is what the word God means. And if that word has not much meaning for you, translate it, and speak of the depths of your life, of the source of your being, of your ultimate concern, of what you take seriously without any reservation .... Perhaps you should call this depth hope, simply hope."
~ Paul Tillich, *The Shaking of the Foundations*

January 31st *Hallelujah – Leonard Cohen*
"The life of faith is nothing but the continual pursuit of God through everything that disguises, disfigures, destroys, and, so to say, annihilates him."
~ Jean-Pierre de Caussade
Abandonment to Divine Providence

FEBRUARY: DEPRESSION

February 1ˢᵗ *Little Boxes – Pete Seeger*
"Faces along the bar
Cling to their average day:
The lights must never go out,
The music must always play,
All the conventions conspire
To make this fort assume
The furniture of home;
Lest we should see where we are,
Lost in a haunted wood,
Children afraid of the night
Who have never been happy or good."
  ~ W.H. Auden, "September 1, 1939"

February 2ⁿᵈ *Life Ain't Easy – Dr. Hook*
"But beware the once-born psychological cheerleaders, the purveyors of one-minute solutions, who assure you that all you need to do is change your diet, manage your time more efficiently, exercise more, learn to relax on the job, adjust your priorities, communicate better, learn to enjoy stress, or think positively and avoid 'negative' emotions. Because stress is not simply a disease; it is a symptom that you are living someone else's life, marching to a drumbeat that doesn't syncopate with your personal body rhythms, playing a role you didn't create, living a script written by an alien authority. Depression is more than low self-esteem; it is a distant early warning that you are on the wrong path and that

something in you is being pressed down, beat on, kept imprisoned, dishonored. Burnout is nature's way of telling you you've been going through the motions but your soul has departed; you're a zombie, a member of the walking dead, a sleepwalker."

~ Sam Keen, *Fire in the Belly: On Being a Man*

February 3rd *Boulevard Of Broken Dreams – Tony Bennett*
"To live illusionless, in the abandoned mine / shaft of doubt, and still / mime illusions for others? A puzzle / for the maker who has thought / once too often too coldly. / Since I was more than a child / trying on a thousand faces / I have wanted one thing: to know / simply as I know my name / at any given moment, where I stand. / How much expense of time and skill / which might have set itself / to angelic fabrications! All merely / to chart one needle in the haymow? / Find yourself and you find the world? / Solemn presumption! Mighty Object / no one but itself has missed, / what's lost, if you stay lost? Someone / ignorantly loves you – will that serve? / Shrug that off, and presto! – / the needle drowns in the haydust. / Think of the whole haystack – / a composition so fortuitous / it only looks monumental. / There's always a straw twitching somewhere. / Wait out the long chance, and / your needle too could get nudged up / to the apex of that bristling calm. / Rusted, possibly. You might not want / to swear it was the Object, after all. / Time wears us old utopians. / I no longer think / 'truth' is the most beautiful of words. / Today, when I see

'truthful' / written somewhere, it flares / like a white orchid in wet woods, / rare and grief-delighting, up from the page. / Sometimes, unwittingly even, / we have been truthful. / In a random universe, what more/ exact and starry consolation? / Don't think I think / facts serve better than ignorant love. / Both serve, and still / our need mocks our gear."
~ Adrienne Rich, "Double Monologue"

February 4th *A Stranger On Earth - Marianne Faithfull*
"How weary, stale, flat, and unprofitable,
Seem to me all the uses of this world."
~ William Shakespeare, *Hamlet*

February 5th *Desperado – The Eagles*
"To the degree that we are faulted, we are motivated by our fear of deficiency rather than our trust in sufficiency. Our love proceeds more from trying to fill the hole than by allowing the whole to fill us. We become obsessed with what is missing rather than what is given, with the past rather than the present, with the wound rather than the gift."
~ Sam Keen, *The Passionate Life: Stages of Loving*

February 6th *Isolation – John Lennon*
"We wear the mask that grins and lies,
If hides our cheeks and shades our eyes
This debt we pay to human guile;
With torn and bleeding hearts we smile
And mouth with myriad subtleties

Why should the world be over-wise,
In counting all our tears and sighs?
Nay, let them only see us, while
We wear the mask.
We smile, but oh great Christ, our cries
To Thee from tortured souls arise.
We sing, by oh the clay is vile
Beneath our feet, and long the mile;
But let the world dream otherwise,
We wear the mask."
~ Paul Laurence Dunbar, "We Wear The Mask"

February 7th *I Am a Rock – Simon & Garfunkel*
"If an individual's self-system is sensitive, flexible, and open to influences from the world around her and from her inner emotional life, she will adapt to new circumstances by spontaneously evolving a new optimal order. However, the less open an individual's self-system, the more rigid will be her way or ordering her view of the world. Her self-image will be narrow, and she will not integrate unacceptable emotions and rejected aspects of her personality into her self-system. A depressed person's world is static, maladaptive, and closed. She may be so withdrawn and isolated from life that she rarely experiences chaos because she is defended against it. She drains herself of energy through her desperate efforts to avoid and reject experiences of chaos. By rejecting the realities of human existence and withdrawing emotionally, she restricts the full development of her personality. Such a person is limited

in her awareness of what is happening both inside and outside herself. She is less in touch with her needs and desires and, therefore, less able to satisfy them."
 ~ Andrea Nelson, *Sacred Sorrows*

February 8th *Wish You Were Here – Pink Floyd*
"The absurd is born of the confrontation between the human call and the unreasonable silence of the world."
 ~ Albert Camus, *The Myth of Sisyphus*

February 9th *Hey You – Pink Floyd*
"We are the hollow men
We are the stuffed men
Leaning together
Headpiece filled with straw, Alas!
Our dried voices, when
We whisper together
Are quiet and meaningless
As wind in dry grass
Or rat's feet over broken glass
In our dry cellar
Shape without form, shade without colour,
Paralyzed force, gesture without motion;
Those who have crossed
With direct eyes, to death's other kingdom
Remember us – if at all – not as lost
Violent souls, but only
As the hollow men
The stuffed men... Here we go round the prickly pear
Prickly pear prickly pear

Here we go round the prickly pear
At five o' clock in the morning
Between the idea
And the reality
Between the motion
And the act
Falls the shadow
For Thine is the Kingdom
Between the conception
And the creation
Between the emotion
And the response
Falls the shadow
Life is very long
Between the desire
And the spasm
Between the potency
And the existence
Between the essence
And the descent
Falls the shadow
For Thine is the Kingdom
For Thine is
Life is
For Thine is the
This is the way the world ends
This is the way the world ends
This is the way the world ends
Not with a bang but a whimper."
 ~ T.S. Eliot, "The Hollow Men"

February 10th *Comfortably Numb – Pink Floyd*

"It is extraordinary how we go through life with eyes half shut, with dull ears, with dormant thoughts. Perhaps it is just as well; and it may be that it is this very dullness that makes life to the incalculable majority so supportable and so welcome."

~ Joseph Conrad, *Lord Jim*

February 11th *Hurt – Johnny Cash*

"There I walked, and there I raged;
The spiritual savage caged
Within my skeleton raged afresh
To feel, behind a carnal mesh,
The clean bones crying in the flesh."

~ Elinor Wylie, "Full Moon"

February 12th *Loser – 3 Doors Down*

"But the wilderness had found him out early, and had taken on him a terrible vengeance for the fantastic invasion. I think it had whispered to him things about himself which he did not know, things of which he had no conception till he took counsel with this great solitude – and the whisper had proved irresistibly fascinating. It echoed loudly within him because he was hollow at the core."

~ Joseph Conrad, *The Heart of Darkness*

February 13th *I See A Darkness – Johnny Cash*

"In a dark time, the eye begins to see,
I meet my shadow in the deepening shade;

I hear my echo in the echoing wood –
A lord of nature weeping to a tree.
I live between the heron and the wren,
Beasts of the hill and serpents of the den.
What's madness but nobility of soul
At odds with circumstance? The day's on fire!
I know the purity of pure despair,
My shadow pinned against a sweating wall.
That place among the rocks – is it a cave,
Or winding path? The edge is what I have.
A steady storm of correspondences!
A night flowing with birds, a ragged moon,
And in broad day the midnight come again!
A man goes far to find out what he is –
Death of the self in a long, tearless night,
All natural shapes blazing unnatural light.
Dark, dark my light, and darker my desire.
My soul, like some heat-maddened summer fly,
Keeps buzzing at the sill. Which I is I?
A fallen man, I climb out of my fear.
The mind enters itself, and God the mind,
And one is One, free in the tearing wind."
   ~ Theodore Roethke, "In a Dark Time"

February 14th *Beware Of Darkness – George Harrison*
"It is not upon you alone the dark patches fall, / The dark threw its patches down on me also, / The best I had done seemed to me blank and suspicious, / My great thoughts as I supposed them, were they not in reality meager?"   ~ Walt Whitman, "Leaves of Grass"

February 15th *Sound Of Silence – Simon & Garfunkel*

"His harvest is a quiet mind which he prefers to being possessed by God, as he prefers comfort to pleasure, convenience to liberty, and a pleasant temperature to that deathly inner consuming fire."

~ Herman Hesse, *Steppenwolf*

February 16th *Eclipse – John Denver*

"If any one idea captures the essence of how the alienated person perceives the world, it is flatness. The world goes flat because withdrawal from the world is at the same time a withdrawal of the projected meanings (cognitive intentions) and values (cathexes) by which we interpret and enliven the world. Accordingly, when alienation sets in, the world begins to lose all modes and gradations of lived depth. It loses its peaks and valleys, challenges and disappointments, profundities and banalities, heroes and fools. It becomes a world in which everything is 'equal' in the sense of being equally shallow, neutral, and gray. Actions become 'equal' because they are all reduced to mere motions. And persons become 'equal' because they are all reduced to mere personas. The world of the alienated person becomes flat throughout, for in withdrawing from the world the alienated persons ceases intersecting in depth with the world."

~ Michael Washburn, *Sacred Sorrows*

February 17th *Tomorrow Is Today – Billy Joel*

"Tomorrow, or the day after, the world would be good

again, it would be wonderful. At least it was so until the sadness returned, the brooding, the remorse for dying fish and wilting flowers, the horror of insensitive, pig-like, staring-but-not-seeing human existence."
~ Herman Hesse, *Narcissus and Goldmund*

February 18th *Helpless – Neil Young*
"But what am I?
An infant crying in the night;
An infant crying for the light,
And with no language but a cry."
~ Alfred, Lord Tennyson, "In Memoriam A.H.H."

February 19th *4+20 – Stephen Stills*
"That life is worth living is the most necessary of assumptions, and, were it not assumed, the most impossible of conclusions."
~ George Santayana, *The Life of Reason*

February 20th *Outside the Wall – Pink Floyd*
"I, fed with judgment, in a fleshly tomb, am
Buried above ground."
~ William Cowper
"Lines Written During a Period of Insanity"

February 21st *Vincent - Don McLean*
"True, he had made that last stride, he had stepped over the edge, while I had been permitted to draw back my hesitating foot. And perhaps in this is the whole difference; perhaps all the wisdom, and all truth, and all

sincerity, are just compressed into that inappreciable moment of time in which we step over the threshold of the invisible. Perhaps! I like to think my summing-up would not have been a word of careless contempt. Better his cry – much better. It was an affirmation, a moral victory paid for by innumerable defeats, by abominable terrors, by abominable satisfactions. But it was a victory!"

~ Joseph Conrad, *The Heart of Darkness*

February 22nd *Dust In The Wind - Kansas*
"Pile the bodies high at Austerlitz and Waterloo,
Shovel them under and let me work –
I am the grass, I cover all."

~ Carl Sandburg, "Grass"

February 23rd *All Things Must Pass - George Harrison*
"Margaret, are you grieving
Over Goldengrove unleaving?
Leaves, Like the things of man, you
With your fresh thoughts care for, can you?
Ah! As the heart grows older
It will come to such sights colder
By and by, nor spare a sigh
Though worlds of wanwood leafmeal lie;
And yet you will weep and know why.
Now no matter, child, the name
Sorrow's springs are the same.
Nor mouth had, no nor mind, expressed
What heart heard of, ghost guessed:

It is the blight man was born for,
It is Margaret you mourn for."
~ Gerald Manley Hopkins
"Spring and Fall: To a Young Child"

February 24th *Reflections Of My Life - Marmalade*
"Tomorrow, and tomorrow, and tomorrow,
Creeps in this petty pace from day to day,
To the last syllable of recorded time,
And all of our yesterdays have lighted fools
The way to dusty death. Out, out brief candle!
Life's but a walking shadow, a poor player
That struts and frets his hour upon the stage,
And then is heard no more: it is a tale
Told by an idiot, full of sound and fury,
Signifying nothing."
~ William Shakespeare, *Macbeth*

February 25th *Everybody Hurts - REM*
"And thinking over the long pilgrimage of his past he accepted it joyfully. He accepted the deformity which had made life so hard for him; he knew that it had warped his character, but now he also saw that by reason of it he had acquired that power of introspection which had given him so much delight. Without it he would never have had his keen appreciation of beauty, his passion for art and literature, and his interest in the varied spectacle of life. The ridicule and the contempt which had so often been heaped upon him had turned his mind inward and called forth those flowers which he

felt would never lose their fragrance. Then he saw that the normal was the rarest thing in the world. Everybody had some defect, of body or of mind...At this moment he could feel a holy compassion for them all."

~ W. Somerset Maugham, *Of Human Bondage*

February 26th *I Shall Be Released – The Band*
"After hours of careful listening, my therapist offered an image that helped me eventually reclaim my life. 'You seem to look upon depression as the hand of an enemy trying to crush you,' he said, 'Do you think you could see it instead as the hand of a friend, pressing you down to ground on which it is safe to stand?'... The spiritual journey is full of paradoxes. One of them is that the humiliation that brings us down – down to the ground on which it is safe to stand and to fall – eventually takes us to a firmer sense of self."

~ Parker J. Palmer, *Let Your Life Speak*

February 27th *Hard Times Come Again – Mavis Staples*
"Yet through depression we enter depths and in depths find soul. Depression is essential to the tragic sense of life...It brings refuge, limitation, focus, gravity, weight, and humble powerlessness. It reminds of death. The true revolution begins in the individual who can be true to his or her depression. Neither jerking oneself out of it, caught in cycles of hope and despair, nor suffering through it till it turns, nor theologizing it – but discovering the consciousness and depths it wants. So begins the revolution in behalf of soul."

~ James Hillman, *Re-Visioning Psychology*

February 28th *Trouble In Mind – Nina Simone*
"Don't run away from grief , o soul
Look for the remedy inside the pain.
because the rose came from the thorn
and the ruby came from a stone."
~ Rumi

February 29th *Melody Cool – Mavis Staples*
"Is life so wretched? Isn't rather your hands which are
too small, your vision which is muddled? You are the
one which must grow up."
~ Dag Hammarskjold, *Markings*

MARCH: TRANSFORMATION

March 1ˢᵗ *Got To Begin Again – Billy Joel*
"Well mythology tells us that where you stumble, there your treasure is… And where it seems most challenging lies the greatest invitation to find deeper and greater powers in ourselves. Toynbee speaks of challenge and response, and every culture and individual runs into these challenges… But where the power to respond succeeds, there comes a new amplification of life and consciousness."
   ~ Joseph Campbell, *An Open Life*

March 2ⁿᵈ *Everything Must Change – Nina Simone*
"All changes, even the most longed for, have their melancholy; for what we leave behind us is a part of ourselves; we must die to one life before we can enter another."
   ~ Anatole France

March 3ʳᵈ *Change – Blind Melon*
"Hence Kierkegaard and Nietzsche and Camus and Sartre have proclaimed that courage is not the absence of despair; it is, rather, the capacity to move ahead in spite of despair… A chief characteristic of this courage is that it requires a centeredness within our own being, without which we would feel ourselves to be a vacuum. The 'emptiness' within corresponds to an apathy without; and apathy adds up, in the long run, to cowardice. That is why we must always base our

commitment in the center of our own being, or else no commitment will be ultimately authentic… In human beings courage is necessary to make being and becoming possible. An assertion of the self, a commitment, is essential if the self is to have any reality."

~ Rollo May, *The Courage to Create*

March 4th *Times Like These – Foo Fighters*
"The search for order, for unity, for wholeness is, I believe, a motivating force of signal importance in the lives of men and women of every variety of temperament…But the greater the disharmony within, the sharper the spur to seek harmony, or, if one has the gifts, to create harmony.

~ Anthony Storr, *Solitude: A Return to Self*

March 5th *The Show Must Go On - Queen*
"Out of the night that covers me,
Black as the pit from pole to pole,
I thank whatever gods may be,
For my unconquerable soul."

~ William Ernest Henley, "Invictus"

March 6th *Cool Change – Little River Band*
"Chaos theory focuses on the dynamics of the system as a whole, on what the parts are doing all together, rather than individually. It challenges us to see the universe as a spontaneous, flowing, whole process, an interconnecting web of relationships. Such a world view

discourages us from seeing depression as an isolated, totally undesirable symptom to be alleviated as soon as possible. Instead we are compelled to wonder how depression fits into the overall process of change. In the human psyche, tempestuous emotional states generate a creative tension between chaos and order that is vital to the richly complex process of human psychological growth...When we accept the transformative potential of chaos, we often find that our original difficulties were caused by our clinging inflexibly to our habitual way of ordering our world. We seek security in order, but often such a prevailing order is intolerant of new input and rejects chaos that threatens to bring disorder to our psyche. When we protect ourselves from chaos we cut ourselves off from the flow of life. Eventually this may precipitate depression. Learning to face chaos is an integral step on the way to transforming depression into a new, more adaptive order."
~ Andrea Nelson, *Sacred Sorrows*

March 7th *Change Is Gonna Come – Sam Cooke*
"You must be the change you want to see in the world."
~ Mahatma Gandhi

March 8th *I Wish I Knew How It Would Feel To Be Free – Nina Simone*
"Suffice it to say that [Kierkegaard] believed that inner conflict and guilt feeling are always a concommitant of creativity... These are not to be termed neurotic, nor do they result in neurotic anxiety so long as the individual

can confront his creative crises and resolve them for further expansion of the self. For example, every creative possibility in individual development involves some killing of the past, some breaking of past forms or patterns; to move ahead raises the unavoidable spectre of isolation from one's fellows and one's previous patterns; one is tempted to remain in the familiar and the safe, not to venture. But one achieves selfhood only by moving ahead, despite conflict, guilt, isolation, and anxiety. If one does not move ahead, the result is ultimately neurotic anxiety. For Kierkegaard, neurotic anxiety is the result of retrenchment, which occurs because the person is afraid of freedom."

~ Rollo May, *Psychology and the Human Dilemma*

March 9th *We Shall Overcome – SNCC Freedom Singers*
"It is now or never, the hour of the knife,
The break with the past, the major operation."
~ C. Day Lewis
"Consider These, For We Have Condemned Them"

March 10th *Keep on Pushing – Curtis Mayfield*
"To transform opposition into paradox is to allow both sides of an issue, both pairs of opposites, to exist in equal dignity and worth...If I can stay with my conflicting impulses long enough, the two opposing forces will teach each other something and produce an insight that serves them both. This is not compromise but a depth of understanding that puts my life in perspective and allows me to know with certainty what I

should do."
~ Robert A. Johnson, *Owning Your Own Shadow*

March 11th *Move On Up – Curtis Mayfield*
"It lies in our very nature to be on-the-way. We strive to cut across time. That is possible only in polarities: only when we exist entirely in this time of our historicity can we experience something of the eternal present. Only as determinant men, each in his specificity, can we experience humanity as such… We are creatures of this sort, and we are lost if we relinquish our orientation to the dry land. But we are not content to remain there."
~ Karl Jaspers, *The Way to Wisdom*

March 12th *Place In The Sun – Stevie Wonder*
"There is in this world no such force as the force of a person determined to rise. The human soul cannot be permanently chained."
~ W.E.B. DuBois

March 13th *Ooh Child – Five Stairsteps*
"Try to love the questions themselves, like the locked rooms and like books written in a foreign language. Do not now look for the answers. They cannot now be given to you because you could not live with them. It is a question of experiencing everything. At present you need to live the question. Perhaps you will gradually, without even noticing it, find yourself experiencing the answer, some distant day."
~ Rainer Maria Rilke, *Letters to a Young Poet*

March 14th *Only the Strong Survive — Jerry Butler*
"Don't wish it were easier, wish you were better. Don't wish for fewer problems, wish for more skills. Don't wish for less challenges, wish for more wisdom."
~ John Earl Shoaff

March 15th *Keep On Smilin' — Wet Willie*
"Rumi does not resolve contradictions so much as he sings them. He lives in them. Incarnation is not a dungeon, but a closed box of musk getting muskier. The smallness of the play area is a strength! Particles turning in tiny orbits compose the diamond we inhabit. Rumi is in these poems, enduring and enjoying the many contradictions: the sweetness of grief, the freedom of limits, the warmth of going naked, the eloquent silence."
~ *Rumi: The Glance* translated by Coleman Barks

March 16th *It Don't Come Easy — Ringo Starr*
"If it were not for reality, I would be perfectly all right."
~ Karen Horney, *Neurosis and Human Growth*

March 17th *Better Things — The Kinks*
"When half-gods go,
The gods arrive."
~ Ralph Waldo Emerson, "Give All to Love"

March 18th *Don't Stop — Fleetwood Mac*
"The essence of a healthy emotional and mental life is action and decision making taking conscious control of your own destiny. This is not accomplished by refusing

action. Similarly, one's own inner development, which exists in relation to others and the cosmos as well as to the self, is not furthered by a retreat from this relationship."

~ Lawrence LeShan, *How to Meditate*

March 19th *Get on Your Feet – Gloria Estefan*
"When I think of nourishing the soul, I think of nurturing the ability to respond positively to life – that is, the ability to sustain passion for our interests, values, and projects. I believe that the worst of all spiritual defeats is to lose enthusiasm for life's possibilities… Two things are needed: an ability to appreciate the positives in our life – and a commitment to action. Every day, it's important to ask and answer these questions: "What's good in my life?" and "What needs to be done?" The first question keeps us focused on positives; the second keeps us proactive and reminds us that we are responsible for our own happiness and well-being."

~ Nathaniel Branden, *The Handbook of the Soul*

March 20th *Life Is a Song Worth Singing – Teddy Pendergrass*
"Man is still responsible. He must turn the alloy of modern experience into the steel of mastery and character. His success lies not within the stars but within himself. He must carry on the fight of self-correction and discipline. He must fight mediocrity as sin and live against the imperative of life's highest ideals."   ~ Frank Curtis Williams

March 21ˢᵗ *I'll Begin Again – Sammy Davis, Jr.*

"Appearances notwithstanding, despair is not an utterly negative condition. It is a condition astir with positive possibilities. For the process of dying to the world that leads to despair stimulates a yearning for life that, unbeknownst to the despairing person, draws on hidden spiritual resources… Few people follow the path discussed in this essay all the way to the limit point of despair… For [those who do], the old self does not bounce back; it dies and therefore makes way for the birth of a new self. This new self is a self born of faith, a spiritual self that knows that fulfillment arises from within and therefore need not be pursued as an outer, worldly goal. Accordingly, although this new self is very much a worldly self in the sense of being actively engaged and completely at home in the world, it is a self whose basic purpose is no longer the pursuit of worldly goals. It is a self whose basic purpose is, rather, to grow in spirit and to reach out in spirit to others."

~ Michael Washburn, *Sacred Sorrows*

March 22ⁿᵈ *Coming Out of the Dark – Gloria Estefan*

"We cannot emphasize enough that although the experience of nothingness can be a negative experience, it is actually a crucially positive one. Although a person in the throes of nothingness may experience little that makes sense, this seeming absence of meaning is really a quest for the presence of meaning. The apparent loss of meaning in nothingness is actually an active quest for relatedness and fulfillment. The yearning of loneliness is a search for the intimacy of love; the desolation of aloneness is a springboard to the togetherness of love; the emptiness of depression is a quest for the fulfillment of joy; the change of anxiety is a movement toward the permanence of commitment; the groundlessness of dread is a preparation for the solidarity of courage; the burden of guilt is a summons for the lightness of integrity; the shackles of frustration are a plea for the freedom of autonomy; the heat of anger is a purgation for the coolness of serenity; the lethargy of boredom is a thirst for the vitality of enthusiasm; the lifelessness of apathy is a retreat for the re-entry into life; the pain of anguish is a breakdown for the breakthrough of authenticity."

~ William F. Kraft, *The Psychology of Nothingness*

March 23rd *I Made It Through the Rain – Barry Manilow*
"According to the theory proposed here, anxiety is understandably a concomitant of the shaking of the self-world relationship that occurs in the encounter. Our sense of identity is threatened; the world is not as we experienced it before, and since self and world are always correlated, we no longer are what we were before. Past, present, and future form a new Gestalt... The anxiety we feel is temporary rootlessness, disorientation; it is the anxiety of nothingness. Creative people, as I see them, are distinguished by the fact that they can live with anxiety, even though a high price may be paid in terms of insecurity, sensitivity, and defenselessness for the gift of 'divine madness,' to

borrow the term used by the classical Greeks. They do not run away from non-being, but by encountering and wrestling with it, force it to produce being. They knock on silence for an answering music; they pursue meaninglessness until they can force it to mean."

~ Rollo May, *The Courage to Create*

March 24th *Back In Business – Liza Minnelli*
"Success is counted sweetest
By those who ne'er succeed.
To comprehend a nectar
Requires sorest need."

~ Emily Dickinson, "Success"

March 25th *Get Happy – Ella Fitzgerald*
"Joy is altogether beyond any consideration of pleasure or pain, and in fact requires a knowledge and acceptance of pain. Joy is the reaction one has to the full appreciation of Being. It is one's response to finding one's rightful, rooted place in life, and it can happen only when one knows through and through that absolutely nothing is being denied or otherwise shut out of awareness." ~ Gerald G. May, *Will & Spirit*

March 26th *There Will Be Some Changes Made-Delores Gray*
"To dispose a soul to action, we must upset its equilibrium." ~ Eric Hoffer, *The Ordeal of Change*

March 27th *Pick Yourself Up – Diana Krall*
"If you don't like what you are doing, you can always

pick up your needle and move to another groove."
~ Timothy Leary

March 28th *Yes I Can –Sammy Davis, Jr.*
"But if a person has had the sense of the Call-the feeling that there's an adventure for him- and if he doesn't follow that, but remains in the society because it is safe and secure, then life dries up… If you have the guts to follow the risk, however, life opens, opens, opens up all along the line… I feel that if one follows what I call one's 'bliss' – the thing that really gets you deep in the gut and that you feel is your life- doors will open up. They do!"
~ Joseph Campbell, *An Open Life*

March 29th *New Attitude – Patti LaBelle*
"As an open system, a person is linked with her environment in a multitude of complex and interconnected ways. Each transformation to a higher level of organization and complexity creates more points of contact both within a person and between her and the environment. As an individual's sense of self becomes more complexly organized, she has access to wider and deeper ranges of environments from which to draw energy and into which to dissipate wasted energy or entropy. There is a greater flow of energy through the system. She is more engaged in the world and more aware of her inner experiences; therefore, she is more open to perturbations that destabilize her self-system and trigger further growth. Transformation

expands boundaries that constrain our behavior and our ways of defining ourselves as we break out of old restricting attitudes and qualities."

~ Andrea Nelson, *Sacred Sorrows*

March 30th *I'm Still Standing – Elton John*
"A man learns to skate by staggering about making a fool of himself; indeed, he progresses in all things by making a fool of himself."

~ George Bernard Shaw

March 31st *Tubthumping - Chumbawamba*
"Fall seven times, stand up eight."

~ Japanese proverb

APRIL: EMERGENCE

April 1ˢᵗ *Here Comes the Sun – Nina Simone*
"Awake!
The sun rises in the east.
At the ocean,/ the deep ocean,
Climb to the heavens,
highest heaven.
In the east,
is the sun.
Rise! Awake!"
~ Hawaiian chant, "E ala e"

April 2ⁿᵈ *To The Morning – Dan Fogelberg*
"He has, in a word, awakened with tremulous awe to the discovery that his life which he has hitherto believed limited and confined to what he knew, reaches infinitely beyond his knowledge and is far greater than he ever dreamed."
~ Basil William Maturin
Self-Knowledge and Self-Discipline

April 3ʳᵈ *In the Morning of My Life - Lulu*
"A lifestyle is an art form. It brings life and wonder, joy and hope to persons otherwise condemned to superficial living. Our times call for the creation of lifestyles of spiritual substance."
~ Matthew Fox
The Coming of the Cosmic Christ

April 4th *Morning Has Broken – Cat Stevens*

"Lord, the air smells good today, / straight from the mysteries / within the inner courts of God. / A grace like new clothes thrown / across the garden, free medicine for everybody. / The trees in their prayer, the birds in praise, / the first blue violets kneeling. / Whatever came from Being is caught up in being, drunkenly / forgetting the way back."

~ Rumi, "Lord, the Air Smells Good Today"

April 5th *Good Morning Starshine – Oliver*

"As to me I know of nothing else but miracles, / Whether I walk the streets of Manhattan, / Or wade with naked feet along the beach just in the edge of the water, / Or the wonderfulness of the sundown, or of the stars shining so quiet and bright, / Or the exquisite delicate thin curve of the new moon in spring; / These with the rest, one and all, are miracles, / The whole referring, yet each distinct and in its place."

~ Walt Whitman, "Miracles"

April 6th *It's A Beautiful Morning – The Rascals*

"My soul is swift upon the wing,
And in its deeps a song I bring;
Come, Love, and we together sing,
"'Tis morning, 'tis morning."

~ Paul Laurence Dunbar, "Morning"

April 7th *There Is Beauty in the World - Macy Gray*

"Our interpretation is that the soul- by the very truth of

its nature, by its affiliation to the noblest Existents in the hierarchy of Being- when it sees anything of that kin, or any trace of that kinship, thrills with an immediate delight, takes its own to itself, and thus stirs anew to the sense of its nature and of all its affinity."
  ~ Plotinus, *Ennead* I.6 [1], "On Beauty"

April 8th *In the Morning When I Rise-Sweet Honey in the Rock*
"Listen to the Exhortation of the Dawn!
Look to this Day!
For it is Life, the very Life of Life.
In its brief course lie all the
Verities and Realities of your Existence.
The Bliss of Growth,
The Glory of Action,
The Splendor of Beauty;
For Yesterday is but a Dream,
And To-morrow is only a Vision;
But To-day well lived makes
Every Yesterday a Dream of Happiness,
And every Tomorrow a Vision of Hope.
Look well therefore to this Day!
Such is the Salutation of the Dawn!"
  ~ Kalidasa, "Exhortation of the Dawn"

April 9th *Daybreak – Barry Manilow*
"And the day came when the risk to remain tight in a bud was more painful than the risk it took to blossom."
  ~ Anais Nin, *Diaries*

April 10th *Let The Day Begin — The Call*
"Let it be spring!
Come, bubbling, surging tide of sap!
Come, rush of creation!
Come, life! surge through this mass of mortification!"
  ~ D.H. Lawrence, "Craving for Spring"

April 11th *Beautiful Day — U2*
"There are only two ways to live your life. One is as though nothing is a miracle. The other is though everything is a miracle."
  ~ Albert Einstein

April 12th *Beautiful Life — Ace of Base*
"Nor sedulous as I have been to trace
How nature by extrinsic passion first
Peopled the mind with forms sublime or fair,
And made me love them, may I here omit
How other pleasures have been mine, and joys
Of subtler origin; how I have felt,
Not seldom even in that tempestuous time,
Those hallowed and pure motions of the sense
Which seem, in their simplicity, to own
An intellectual charm; that calm delight
Which, if I err not, surely must belong
To those first-born affinities that fit
Our new existence to existing things,
And, in our domain of being, constitute
The bond of union between life and joy."
  ~ William Wordsworth, "The Prelude"

April 13th *Alive in the World – Jackson Browne*

"Don't ask what the world needs. Ask what makes you come alive and go do it. Because what the world needs is people who have come alive."   ~ Howard Thurman

April 14th *Born Free – Andy Williams*

"To thy bent mind some relaxation give,
And steal one day out of thy life to live.
Oh happy man, he cries, to whom kind Heaven
Has such a freedom always given
Why, mighty madman, what should hinder thee
From being every day as free?"
   ~ Abraham Cowley, "Ode Upon Liberty"

April 15th *Born To Be Wild - Steppenwolf*

"The decision to become an individual, to allow oneself to be moved by the deepest impulses of the self rather than the social consensus, can only be made with fear and trembling. It is, by definition, a lonely decision. It necessarily involves anxiety and self-doubt. At first it will seem awkward, embarrassing, unnatural, and will require a high degree of painful self-consciousness. One will stumble and fall often. Frequently, the path will disappear into the brambles. The outlaw will often wonder whether asserting the right to know, to taste, to experience, to judge is not an act of arrogance. The individual's way always is an unbeaten path... The trans-moral conscience of the outlaw is the inner voice of a universal community that is struggling to be born."
   ~ Sam Keen, *The Passionate Life*

April 16th *Born to Wander – Rare Earth*
"In the beginner's mind there are many possibilities, in the expert's, there are few."
~ Shunryu Suzuki Rochi, *Zen Mind, Beginner's Mind*

April 17th *Be Young, Be Foolish, Be Happy – The Tams*
"Such a man often doesn't know himself what he might do, but he feels instinctively: yet am I good for something, yet am I aware of some reason for existing! I know that I might be a totally different man! How then can I be useful, how can I be of service! Something is alive in me: what can it be!"
~ Vincent Van Gogh, *Letter to Theo*

April 18th *Oh Very Young – Cat Stevens*
"Then I ran across the old Quaker saying, 'Let your life speak.' I found those words encouraging, and I thought I understood what they meant: 'Let the highest truths and values guide you. Live up to those demanding standards in everything you do'… Today, some thirty years later, "Let your life speak" means something else to me, a meaning faithful both to the ambiguity of those words and to the complexity of my own experience: 'Before you tell your life what you intend to do with it, listen for what it intends to do with you. Before you tell your life what truths and values you have decided to live up to, let your life tell you what truths you embody, what values you represent."
~ Parker J. Palmer, *Let Your Life Speak*

April 19ᵗʰ *Moon River – Andy Williams*
"One doesn't discover new lands without consenting to lose sight of the shore for a very long time."
~ Andre Gide, *The Counterfeiters*

April 20ᵗʰ *Live for Life – Johnny Mathis*
"Life begets life. Energy creates energy. It is by spending oneself that one becomes rich."
~ Sarah Bernhardt

April 21ˢᵗ *Blue Skies – Ella Fitzgerald*
"Glory be to God for dappled things— / For skies of couple-colour as a brinded cow; / For rose-moles all in stipple upon trout that swim; / Fresh-firecoal chestnut-falls; finches' wings; / Landscape plotted and pieced-- fold, fallow, and plough; / And all trades, their gear and tackle and trim. / All things counter, original, spare, strange; / Whatever is fickle, freckled (who knows how?) / With swift, slow; sweet, sour; adazzle, dim; / He fathers-forth whose beauty is past change: Praise Him."   ~ Gerald Manley Hopkins, "Pied Beauty"

April 22ⁿᵈ *I Can See Clearly Now – Jimmy Cliff*
"He who can no longer pause to wonder and stand rapt in awe is as good as dead; his eyes are closed."
~ Albert Einstein, *The World As I See It*

April 23ʳᵈ *Beautiful – Carole King*
"Exuberance is Beauty."
~ William Blake, "The Marriage of Heaven and Hell"

April 24th *Unwritten – Natalie Bedingfield*
"A joyful life is an individual creation which cannot be copied from a recipe."
~ Mihaly Csikszentmihalyi
Flow: The Psychology of Optimal Experience

April 25th *I'm Coming Out – Diana Ross*
"What is man's first duty? The answer is brief: to be himself."
~ Henrik Ibsen, *Peer Gynt*

April 26th *I Have But One Life To Live – Sammy Davis, Jr.*
"Tell me, what is it you plan to do with your one wild and precious life?"
~ Mary Oliver, "The Summer Day"

April 27th *Yes – Liza Minnelli*
"yes is a world
& in this world of
yes live
(skilfully curled)
all worlds"
~ e.e. cummings, "love is a place"

April 28th *Comes Once in a Lifetime – Judy Garland*
"Happy the man, and happy he alone,
He who can call today his own;
He who, secure within, can say
Tomorrow, do thy worst, for I have liv'd today."
~ John Dryden, "Translation of Horace"

April 29th *I'm Not Anyone – Shirley Bassey*
"I am not yet born; O fill me
With strength against those who would freeze my
humanity, would dragoon me into a lethal automation,
would make me a cog in a machine, a thing with
one face, a thing, and against all those
who would dissipate my entirety, would
blow me like a thistle down hither and
thither or hither and thither/ like water held in the
hands would spill me.
Let them not make me a stone and let them not spill me
Otherwise kill me."
  ~ Louis MacNeice, "Prayer Before Birth"

April 30th *Feeling Good – Nina Simone*
"There are moments when the body is as numinous /as
words, days that are the good flesh continuing./Such
tenderness, those afternoons and evenings,/saying
blackberry, blackberry, blackberry."
  ~ Robert Hass, "Meditation at Lagunitas"

MAY: CREATIVITY

May 1ˢᵗ *Mind Excursion- The Tradewinds*
"My mind to me a kingdom is;
Such present joys therein I find,
That it excels all other bliss
That earth affords or grows by kind;
Though much I want which most would have,
Yet still my mind forbids to crave."
 ~ Edward Dyer, "My Mind to Me a Kingdom Is"

May 2ⁿᵈ *Journey to the Center Of Your Mind – Amboy Dukes*
"The overriding aim of these transpersonal techniques is essentially fourfold: (1) To open the compassionate heart to recognize one's own authentic self, which leads to empathetic acceptance of the uniqueness, yet common spirit, of others; (2) To foster creativity by gaining access to recurring archetypal myths that guide humanity to greater wisdom; (3) To open the intuitive 'inner eye' that lifts an individual beyond the constraints of his ordinary senses, opening the visionary capacity latent in us all; (4) To expand consciousness to the point that an individual directly experiences identity with a universal divine Presence."
 ~ John E. Nelson, *Sacred Sorrows*

May 3ʳᵈ *Inner Light – The Beatles*
"So, dear Sir, I can't give you any advice but this: to go into yourself and see how deep the place is from which your life flows; at its source you will find the answer to

the question of whether you must create… Then take that destiny upon yourself, and bear it, its burden and its greatness, without ever asking what reward must come from outside."

~ Rainer Maria Rilke, *Letters to a Young Poet*

May 4ᵗʰ *Tomorrow Never Knows – The Beatles*
"When this breakthrough of a creative insight into consciousness occurs… we wonder why we were so stupid as not to have seen it earlier. The reason, of course, is that we were not psychologically ready to see it. We could not yet intend the new truth or creative form in art or scientific theory. We were not yet open on the level of intentionality. But the 'truth' itself is simply there."

~ Rollo May, *The Courage to Create*

May 5ᵗʰ *Eight Miles High – The Byrds*
"Thanks to art, instead of seeing one world, our own, we see it multiplied and as many original artists as there are, so many worlds are at our disposal."

~ Marcel Proust, *Remembrance of Things Past*

May 6ᵗʰ *Incense & Peppermints – Strawberry Alarm Clock*
"Creativity transforms us from a detached observer of life into a responsible participant."

~ Naylor, Naylor, & Willimon, *The Search for Meaning*

May 7ᵗʰ *Green Tamborine – Lemon Pipers*
"Thought that can merge wholly into feeling, feeling

that can merge wholly into thought – these are the artist's highest joys."

~ Thomas Mann, *Death in Venice*

May 8th *Make Your Own Kind of Music – Mama Cass Elliot*
"A great deal of the work necessary to equip and activate the mind for the spontaneous part of invention must be done consciously and with an effort of will. Mastering accumulated knowledge, gathering new facts, observing, exploring, experimenting, developing technique and skill, sensibility and discrimination, are all more or less conscious and voluntary activities. The sheer labor of preparing technically for creative work, consciously acquiring the requisite knowledge of a medium and skill in its use, is extensive and arduous enough to repel many from achievement."

~ Brewster Ghiselin
The Creative Process

May 9th *Sing – The Carpenters*
"There is, above all, the laughter that comes from the eternal joy of creation, the joy of making the world new, the joy of expressing the inner riches of the soul – laughter from triumphs over pain and hardship in the passion for an enduring ideal, the joy of bringing the light of happiness, of truth and beauty into a dark world. This is divine laughter par excellence."

~ John Elof Boodin
God: A Cosmic Philosophy of Religion

May 10th *Dreamboat Annie - Heart*

"The receptivity of the artist must never be confused with passivity. Receptivity is the artist's holding him – or herself alive and open to hear what being may speak. Such receptivity requires a nimbleness, a fine-honed sensitivity in order to let one's self be the vehicle of whatever vision may emerge. It is the opposite of the authoritarian demands impelled by 'will power'…It requires a high degree of attention… It is an active listening, keyed to hear the answer, alert to see whatever can be glimpsed when the vision or words do come. It is a waiting for the birthing process to begin to move in its own organic time."

~ Rollo May, *The Courage to Create*

May 11th *Daydream- Lovin' Spoonful*

"The dignity of the artist lies in his duty of keeping awake the sense of wonder in the world."

~ G.K. Chesterton, "The Falling Value of Words"
The Illustrated London Times, 5/21/1927

May 12th *Dreamer - Supertramp*

"Art is a kind of innate drive that seizes a human being and makes him its instrument. The artist is not a person endowed with free will who seeks his own ends, but one who allows art to realize its purpose through him. As a human being he may have many moods and a will and personal aims, but as an artist he is a 'man' in a higher sense – he is 'collective man' – one who carries and shapes the unconscious, psychic forms of mankind."

~ Carl Jung, *Modern Man in Search of a Soul*

May 13th *Dream Weaver – Gary Wright*
"If [an artist] insists on making his picture perfect he will probably work the life out of it until it becomes a body with no soul…The soul of a work of art is that spark where the positive current of divinity – defined here as the vision of perfection – makes contact with the negative pole of humanity. Personality health…consists of bearing within us the dialectical tension of perfection and imperfection. The values of human life – creativity, growth, contribution to humanity – come out of the courageous bearing of this tension."
~ Rollo May, *The Springs of Creative Living*

May 14th *Everybody Has a Dream – Billy Joel*
"How are we to differentiate this expression of the artist's sense of his unrealized possibilities from the petulance of incapacity dissatisfied with its lot?… The criterion is proof of production by the artist, if he is able to find himself. But I suspect that he does not always find himself, that he may look in the end like nothing more than an ineffectual misfit."
~ Brewster Ghiselin, *The Creative Process*

May 15th *Dream On - Aerosmith*
"Until one is committed, there is hesitancy, the chance to draw back, always ineffectiveness. Concerning all acts of initiative (and creation), there is one elementary truth

the ignorance of which kills countless ideas and splendid plans: that the moment one definitely commits oneself, the providence moves too. A whole stream of events issues from the decision, raising in one's favor all manner of unforeseen incidents, meetings and material assistance, which no man could have dreamt would have come his way. I learned a deep respect for one of Goethe's couplets: 'Whatever you can do or dream you can, begin it. Boldness has genius, power and magic in it!'"

~ W.H. Murray, *The Scottish Himalaya Expedition*

May 16th *White Rabbit – Jefferson Airplane*

"To be willing to suffer in order to create is one thing; to realize that one's creation necessitates one's suffering, that suffering is one of the greatest of God's gifts, is almost to reach a mystical solution of the problem of evil."

~ J.W.N. Sullivan, *Beethoven - His Spiritual Development*

May 17th *Wild Child – The Doors*

"What is a Poet?... He is a man speaking to men: a man, it is true, endowed with more lively sensibility, more enthusiasm and tenderness, who has a greater knowledge of human nature, and a more comprehensive soul, than are supposed to be common among mankind; a man pleased with his own passions and volitions as manifested in the goings-on of the Universe, and habitually impelled to create them where he does not find them."

~ William Wordsworth
Preface to the 2ⁿᵈ Edition of Lyrical Ballads

May 18ᵗʰ *Logical Song - Supertramp*
"It is often observed that creative people exhibit a childlike quality, a freshness and spontaneity in their perceiving and responding to life. The essence of creativity is retaining the capacity to see life a fresh everyday and therefore to be able to perceive the unexpected, to leap into the unfamiliar, to be open to the novel."
~ Nathaniel Branden, *The Psychology of Romantic Love*

May 19ᵗʰ *I'm Not Like Everybody Else – The Kinks*
"Nobody can be exactly like me. Sometimes even I have trouble doing it."
~ Tallulah Bankhead

May 20ᵗʰ *I've Gotta Be Me – Sammy Davis, Jr.*
"If you ask me what I came to do in this world, I, an artist, I will answer you" 'I am here to live out loud.'"
~ Emile Zola, *Mes haines*

May 21ˢᵗ *I Am What I Am – Shirley Bassey*
"But it is not at all clear that technology and eros are compatible, or can even live without perpetual warfare. The lover, like the poet, is a menace on the assembly line. Eros breaks existing forms and creates new ones and that, naturally, is a threat to technology. Technology requires regularity, predictability, and runs by the clock.

The untamed eros fights against all concepts and confines of time."
~ Rollo May, *Love and Will*

May 22nd *Don't Rain On My Parade – Barbra Streisand*
"Men must live and create. Live to the point of tears."
~ Albert Camus, *Notebooks* 1935-1942

May 23rd *Born to Fly – Sara Evans*
"Even as a child, I began to aspire to live out my entire life as though it were a work of art. And the artist's heart of enthusiasm and passion for life still beats within me to this day. I see life as a series of choices that can either rob me of my idealism and optimism, or empower me with lasting passion and expectation."
~ Thomas Kinkade, *The Art of Creative Living*

May 24th *I Sing the Body Electric - Fame*
"Where there is no vitality, there is no creativity. Where there is no burning curiosity, there is no creativity. Work is not incubated; the alive, energetic person incubates work. Work is not prepared; the obsessed artist works incessantly, in and out of her own conscious awareness, on problems and melodies, sentences and atmospheric effects, tonalities and passages. If you would like to be creative, you must come alive."
~ Eric Maisel, *Fearless Creating*

May 25th *We Are All Made Of Stars - Moby*
"Man unites himself with the world in the process of

creation."
  ~ Erich Fromm, *The Art of Loving*

May 26th *Shine On You Crazy Diamond – Pink Floyd*
"Every creation springs from abundance. The gods create from an excess of power, an overflow of energy. Creation is accomplished by a surplus of ontological substance."
  ~ Mircea Eliade, *The Sacred and the Profane*

May 27th *Shine – Collective Soul*
"Eckhart is here recognizing a paradox that is inherent in human existence. The potentials and aspirations that work in the depth of a person require outward expression in order for them to fulfill themselves. The imagery of the psyche requires an outer object in which it can concretize itself and in which it can be lived. Without this outer embodiment it would remain an image and an unlived potentiality that did not have the flesh and bones of life. And yet, when the psyche moves to make its vision concrete, it inevitably constricts itself and reduces the divinity that lies dormant within it."
  ~ Ira Progoff
  The Dynamics of Hope and the Image of Utopia

May 28th *Shining Star – Earth, Wind & Fire*
"The first thing we notice in a creative act is that it is an encounter… As I would put it, [true artists] are the ones who enlarge human consciousness… Escapist creativity is that which lacks encounter… This leads us to the

second element in the creative act – namely, the intensity of the encounter... By whatever name one calls it, genuine creativity is characterized by an intensity of awareness, a heightened consciousness... Nietzsche, in his important book The Birth of Tragedy, cites the Dionysian principle of surging vitality with the Apollonian principle of form and rational order as the two dialectical principles that operate in creativity... Ecstasy is the accurate term for the intensity of consciousness that occurs in the creative act. But it is not to be thought of merely as a Bacchic 'letting go'; it involves the total person, with the subconscious and unconscious acting in unity with the conscious. It is not, thus, irrational; it is, rather, suprarational. It brings intellectual, volitional, and emotional functions into play all together."

~ Rollo May, *The Courage to Create*

May 29th *Fame/Flashdance – Irene Cara*
"Make a pile of chips. Do something with your wood, or your stone, or your clay and then if it is lousy throw it away. This is better than doing nothing."

~ Abraham Maslow (quoting an anonymous artist)
Eupsychian Management

May 30th *This Little Light of Mine – The Steeles*
"I honestly think in order to be a writer, you have to learn to be reverent. If not, why are you writing? Why are you here? Let's think of reverence as awe, as presence in and openness to the world. The alternative

is that we stultify, we shut down… This is our goal as writers; to help others have this sense of wonder, seeing things anew, things that can catch us off guard, that break in our small, bordered worlds. When this happens, everything feels more spacious… There is ecstasy in paying attention. You can get into a kind of Wordsworthian openness to the world, where you see in everything the essence of holiness, a sign that God is implicit in all of creation… Most things are not that way, that simple and pure, with so much focus given to each syllable of life as life sings itself. But that kind of attention is the prize."

~ Anne Lamott, *Bird by Bird*

May 31st *One Girl Revolution – Superchic*
"Masterpieces are not single and solitary births; they are the outcomes of many years of thinking in common, of thinking by the body of the people, so that the experience of the mass is behind the single voice."

~ Virginia Woolf, *A Room of One's Own*

JUNE: PASSION

June 1ˢᵗ *Being Alive – Patti LuPone*
"Natures of your kind, with strong delicate senses, the soul-oriented, the dreamers, poets, lovers are almost always superior to us creatures of the mind. You take your being from your mothers. You live fully; you were endowed with the strength of love, the ability to feel. Whereas we creatures of reason, we don't live fully; we live in an arid land, even though we seem to guide and rule you. Yours is the plentitude of life, the sap of the fruit, the garden of passion, the beautiful landscape of art. Your home is the earth; ours is the world of ideas. You are in danger of drowning in the world of the senses; ours is the danger of suffocating in an airless void. You are an artist; I am a thinker. You sleep at the mother's breast; I wake in the desert. For me the sun shines; for you the moon and stars."
~ Herman Hesse, *Narcissus and Goldmund*

June 2ⁿᵈ *I'm Going To Live Until I Die – Frank Sinatra*
"If bursting heart, and maddening brain,
And daring deed, and vengeful steel,
And all that I have felt, and feel,
Betoken love - that love was mine,
And shown by many a bitter sign.
'Tis true, I could not whine nor sigh,
I knew but to obtain or die.
I die - but first I have possessed,
And come what may, I have been blessed."

~ Lord Byron, "The Graour"

June 3rd *A Lot of Livin' To Do —Sammy Davis, Jr.*
"There is only one way to be prepared for death: to be sated. In the soul, in the heart, in the spirit, in the flesh. To the brim."
~ Henry De Montherlant, *Mars et Vita*

June 4th *I Just Want To Celebrate – Rare Earth*
"Life is but life, and death but death!
Bliss is but bliss, and breath but breath!
And, if indeed, I fail,
At least to know the worst is sweet.
Defeat means nothing but defeat,
No drearier can prevail!"
~ Emily Dickinson, "Rouge Gagne"

June 5th *Can't Keep It In – Cat Stevens*
"Cupbearer, it is morning, fill my cup with wine. / Make haste, the heavenly sphere knows no delay. / Before this transient world is ruined and destroyed, / ruin me with a beaker of rose-tinted wine. / The sun of the wine dawns in the east of the goblet. / Pursue life's pleasure, abandon dreams, / and the day when the wheel makes pitchers of my clay, / take care to fill my skull with wine! / We are not men for piety, penance and preaching / but rather give us a sermon in praise of a cup of clear wine. / Wine-worship is a noble task, O Hafiz; / rise and advance firmly to your noble task."
~ Hafiz

June 6th *Born To Be Alive – Peter Hernandez*

"Being that has soul is living being. Soul is the living thing in man, that which lives of itself and causes life... A certain kind of reasonableness is its advocate, and a certain kind of morality adds its blessing. But to have soul is the whole venture of life, for soul is a life giving daemon who plays his elfin game above and below human existence."

~ Carl Jung, *Archetypes and the Collective Unconscious*

June 7th *I'm Alive - ELO*

"In June, amid the golden fields,
I saw a groundhog lying dead.
Dead lay he; my senses shook,
And mind outshot our naked frailty...
The fever arose, became a flame
And Vigour circumscribed the skies,
Immense energy in the sun,
And through my frame a sunless trembling.
My stick had done nor good nor harm.
And so I left; and I returned
In Autumn strict of eye, to see
The sap gone out of the groundhog,
But the bony sodden hulk remained.
But the year had lost its meaning,
And in intellectual chains
I lost both love and loathing,
Mured up in the wall of wisdom...
It has been three years, now.
There is no sign of the groundhog.

I stood there in the whirling summer,
My hand capped a withered heart,
And thought of China and of Greece,
Of Alexander in his tent;
Of Montaigne in his tower,
Of Saint Theresa in her wild lament."
   ~ Richard Eberhart, "The Groundhog"

June 8th *I Got Life – Hair*
"I believe in the flesh and the appetites,
Seeing, hearing, and feeling are miracles,
and each part and tag of me is a miracle."
   ~ Walt Whitman, "Leaves of Grass"

June 9th *Heatwave – Linda Ronstadt*
"Sex, as they harshly call it,
I fell into this morning
at ten o'clock, a drizzling hour
of traffic and wet newspapers.
I thought of him who yesterday
clearly didn't
turn me into a hot field
ready for plowing,
and longing for that young man
pierced me to the roots
bathing every vein, etc.
All day he appears to me
touchingly desirable,
a prize one could wreck one's peace for.
I'd call it love if love

didn't take so many years
but lust too is a jewel
a sweet flower and what
pure happiness to know
all our high-toned questions
breed in a lively animal."
~ Adrienne Rich, "Two Songs"

June 10th *Burning Love – Elvis Presley*
"Let there be one people
dreaming the divinity in their bodies
and giving birth to it in each other.
Let the wonder entrancing one
quicken the blood of another.
Let the new life stirring in that one
plant a seed in another.
Let what sprouts from the heart of this one
flower in the eye of yet another.
Let the fruit of the passion of that one
fill the emptiness of still another.
Let the lost dreams of every one
settle into the ashes
of what may yet surprise us all.
Let the unexpected flame.
We burn."
~ Allan Schnarr, "We Burn"

June 11th *All or Nothing at All – Frank Sinatra*
"Give all to love;
Obey thy heart;

Friends, kindred, days,
Estate, good fame,
Plans, credit, and the muse;
Nothing refuse."
　~ Ralph Waldo Emerson, "Give All to Love"

June 12th *Power Of My Love – Elvis Presley*
"Passion is the feeling of life wanting to connect with life; life inside us connecting with life outside…Devaluing passion or trying to exclude it from marriage only diminishes the vital spark between a man and a woman that propels their journey forward. This leaves us stuck with a hollow, stagnant form, along with an irresistible urge to break out of its constraints."
　~ John Welwood, *Journey of the Heart*

June 13th *Light My Fire – The Doors*
"Those who restrain desire, do so because theirs is weak enough to be restrained."
　~ William Blake, "The Marriage of Heaven and Hell"

June 14th *Fire – Jimi Hendrx*
"Ecstasy. It was once considered a favor of the gods, a divine gift that could lift mortals out of ordinary reality and into a higher world. The transformative fire of ecstasy would burn away the barriers between ourselves and our souls, bestowing on us a greater understanding of our relation to ourselves and the universe."
　~ Robert A. Johnson
Ecstasy: Understanding the Psychology of Joy

June 15th *Fire – Ohio Players*
"Set your life on fire. Seek those who fan your flames."
   ~ Rumi

June 16th *Some Like It Hot – Robert Palmer*
"Disheveled hair, sweaty, smiling, drunken, and / With a torn shirt, singing, the jug in hand / Narcissus loudly laments, on his lips, alas, alas! / Last night at midnight, came and sat right by my bed-stand / Brought his head next to my ears, with a sad song / Said, O my old lover, you are still in dreamland / The lover who drinks this nocturnal brew / Infidel, if not worships the wine's command / Go away O hermit, fault not the drunk / Our Divine gift from the day that God made sea and land / Whatever He poured for us in our cup, we just drank / If it was a cheap wine or heavenly brand / The smile on the cup's face and Beloved's hair strand / Break many who may repent, just as Hafiz falsely planned."
   ~ Hafiz, "Ghazal 26"

June 17th *Lay Your Hands on Me – Peter Gabriel*
"As our blood labors to beget
Spirits, as like souls as it can,
Because such fingers need to knit
That subtle knot, which makes us man;
So must pure lovers' soul descend
To affections, and to faculties
Which sense may reach and apprehend,
Else a great prince in prison lies.

To our bodies turn we then, that so
Weak men on love revealed may look;
Love's mysteries in souls do grow,
But yet – the body is his book.
And if some lover, such as we,
Have heard this dialogue of one,
Let him still mark us, he shall see
Small change when we're to bodies gone."
    ~ John Donne, "The Ecstasy"

June 18th *See Me, Feel Me – The Who*
"My belief is in the blood and flesh as being wiser than the intellect. The body-conscious is where life bubbles up in us. It is how we know we are alive, alive to the depths of our souls, and in touch somewhere with the vivid reaches of the cosmos." ~ D.H. Lawrence

June 19th *Love is Alive – Gary Wright*
"With passion pray.
With passion make love.
With passion eat and drink and dance and play.
Why look like a dead fish
in this ocean of God?"
    ~ Rumi, "With Passion"

June 20th *So Alive – Love & Rockets*
"The living soul demands life, the living soul will not submit to mechanism, the living soul must be regarded with suspicion."
    ~ Feodor Dostoevsky, *Crime and Punishment*

June 21st *Alive & Kicking – Simple Minds*
"For 'eros is a daimon,' we recall; eros has to do not simply with love but with hate also, it has to do with an energizing, a shocking of our normal existence – it is a gadfly which keeps us forever awake; eros is the enemy of nirvana, the breathless peace."
~ Rollo May, *Love and Will*

June 22nd *Livin' La Vida Loca – Ricky Martin*
"Her embrace was an immense press
To print him into her bones
His smiles were the garrets of a fairy palace
Where the real world would never come
Her smiles were spider bites
So he would lie still till she felt hungry
His words were occupying armies
Her laughs were an assassin's attempts
His looks were bullets daggers of revenge
His glances were ghosts in the corner with horrible secrets His whispers were whips and jackboots
Her kisses were lawyers steadily writing
His caresses were the last hooks of a castaway
Her love-tricks were the grinding of locks
And their deep cries crawled over the floors
Like an animal dragging a great trap
His promises were the surgeon's gag
Her promises took the top off his skull
She would get a brooch made of it
His vows pulled out all her sinews
He showed her how to make a love-knot

Her vows put his eyes in formalin
At the back of her secret drawer
Their screams stuck in the wall
Their heads fell apart into sleep like the two halves
Of a lopped melon, but love is hard to stop
In their entwined sleep they exchanged arms and legs
In their dreams their brains took each other hostage
In the morning they wore each other's face."
 ~ Ted Hughes, "Lovesong"

June 23rd *Mysterious Ways – U2*
"Moments of deep sexual intimacy generate a powerful transfusion of energy from a level beyond our familiar ways of relating. As a man becomes pure male, a woman, pure female, the god and goddess enter…In lifting us out of the narrow shell of personality, sexual communion puts us in touch with the larger energies of life flowing through our bodies. Thunder, lightning, electricity, rain, moonlight, and sunshine - the lovers who have not felt these energies in their lovemaking have not tasted the full richness of sexual experience. In deep sexual communion, our worldly masks fall away and the living spirit can be felt and shared in its pure form…This blood communion, which allows a man and a woman to discover themselves as god and goddess, is also the sacred base for monogamy. As pure expression of female energy, she is not just one woman, but all women; and when he becomes pure male, he can be all men to her."
 ~ John Welwood, *Journey of the Heart*

June 24th *Sweet Fire of Love – Robbie Robertson*

"Whomever or whatever Aphrodite imbues with beauty is irresistible. A magnetic attraction results, 'chemistry' happens between the two, and they desire union above all else. They feel a powerful urge to get closer, to have intercourse, to consummate – or 'know' the other…While this drive may be purely sexual, the impulse is often deeper, representing an urge that is both psychological and spiritual. Intercourse is synonymous with communication or communion, consummation may speak of an urge toward completion or perfection, union is to join together as one, and to know is to really understand one another."

~Jean Shinoda Bolen, *Goddesses in Everywoman*

June 25th *Wild Horses - U2*

"This is what is the matter with us, we are bleeding at the roots, because we are cut off from the earth and sun and stars, and love is a grinning mockery, because, poor blossom, we plucked it from its stem on the Tree of Life, and expected it to keep on blooming in our civilized vase on the table."

~ D.H. Lawrence, a propos of *Lady Chatterly's Lover*

June 26th *I'm the Only One – Melissa Etheridge*

"Jealousy lives upon doubts. It becomes madness or ceases entirely as soon as we pass from doubt to certainty."

~ Francois de la Rochefoucauld, *Maxims*

June 27th *Blood & Fire – Indigo Girls*

"If you think it long and mad, / the wind of banners / that passes through my life, / and you decide / to leave me at the shore / of the heart where I have roots, / remember / that on that day, / at that hour, / I shall lift my arms / and my roots will set off / to seek another land. / But / if each day, / each hour, / you feel that you are destined for me / with implacable sweetness, / if each day a flower / climbs up to your lips to seek me,/ ah my love, ah my own, / in me all that fire is repeated, / in me nothing is extinguished or forgotten, / my love feeds on your love, beloved, / and as long as you live it will be in your arms / without leaving mine."

~ Pablo Neruda, "If You Forget Me"

June 28th *Rhythm Of The Heat – Peter Gabriel*

"People say that what we're all seeking is a meaning for life… I think that what we're seeking is an experience of being alive, so that our life experiences on the purely physical plane will have resonance within our own innermost being and reality, so that we actually feel the rapture of being alive."

~ Joseph Campbell, *The Power of Myth*

June 29th *Burning Down the House – Talking Heads*

"My candle burns at both ends;
It will not last the night,
But, ah, my foes, and, oh, my friends –
It gives a lovely light."

~ Edna St. Vincent Millay, "First Fig"

June 30th *To Life – Fiddler on the Roof*
"Yes! Life is a banquet and most poor son-of-bitches are starving to death! Live!"
  ~ Lawrence & Lee, *Auntie Mame*

JULY: LOVE

July 1ˢᵗ *Heart Of Gold – Neil Young*
"There's lots of good fish in the sea… maybe… but the vast masses seem to be mackerel or herring, and if you are not a mackerel or herring yourself, you are likely to find very few good fish in the sea."
  ~D.H. Lawrence, *Lady Chatterly's Lover*

July 2ⁿᵈ *Would You Lay With Me In A Field Of Stone – David Allen Cole*
"The point to grasp is that love involves suffering, not just occasionally, accidently, avoidably. Love is not a happy feeling, a form of euphoria: those are epiphenomena. Love means assuming responsibility for another human being…Love of its very nature involves suffering: sharing the sufferings of the loved one and, besides, suffering over the limitations of the other human being, not excluding those of which the loved one is not even conscious. Love is the antithesis of peace."   ~ Walter Kaufman, *The Faith of a Heretic*

July 3ʳᵈ *Love Will Turn You Around – Kenny Rogers*
"Their love was great. Most people experience love without becoming aware of the extraordinary nature of this emotion. But to them…the moments when passion visited their doomed existence like a breath of eternity were moments of revelation, of continually new discoveries about themselves and life."
  ~ Boris Pasternak, *Doctor Zhivago*

July 4ᵗʰ *Love Changes Everything - Sarah Brightman*
"Love is a great force that tears off all masks. And people who run away from love, run away in order to keep their masks."
~ P.D. Ouspensky, *Tertium Organum*

July 5ᵗʰ *Higher Ground – Barbra Streisand*
"That's why it's a sacrament: you give up your personal simplicity to participate in a relationship. And when you're giving, you're not giving to the other person: you're giving to the relationship. And if you realize that you are in the relationship just as the other person is, then it becomes life building, a life fostering and enriching experience, not an impoverishment because you're giving to somebody else…This is the challenge of marriage. What a beautiful thing is a life together as growing personalities, each helping the other to flower, rather than just moving into the standard archetype. It's a wonderful moment when people can make the decision to be something quite astonishing and unexpected, rather than cookie-mold products."
~ Joseph Campbell, *An Open Life*

July 6ᵗʰ *Love Is A Many Splendored Thing – Nat King Cole*
"A Book of Verses underneath the Bough,
A Jug of Wine, a loaf of bread – and Thou
Beside me singing in the Wilderness –
Oh, Wilderness were Paradise enow!"
~ Edward Fitzgerald
"The Rubaiyat of Omar Khayyam"

July 7th *When I Fall In Love – Nat King Cole*
"How many loved your moments of glad grace,
And loved your beauty, with love false or true,
But one man loved the pilgrim soul in you,
And loved the sorrows of your changing face."
    ~ W.B. Yeats, "When You Are Old"

July 8th *Tenderly – Sarah Vaughan*
"somewhere I have never traveled gladly beyond
any experience, your eyes have their silence:
in your most fraile gesture are things which enclose me,
or which I cannot touch because they are too near.
your slightest look easily will enclose me
though I have closed myself as fingers,
you open always petal by petal myself as Spring opens
(touching skillfully, mysteriously) her first rose…
nothing which we are to perceive in this world equals
the power of your intense fragility: whose texture
compels me with the colour of its countries,
rendering death and forever with each breathing
(I do not know what it is about you that closes
and opens; only something in me understands
the voice of your eyes is deeper than all roses)
nobody, not even the rain, has such small hands."
    ~ e.e. cummings
    "somewhere I have never traveled, gladly beyond"

July 9th *I Only Have Eyes For You – The Flamingos*
"In their choice of lovers, both the male and female
reveal their essential nature. The type of human being

which we prefer reveals the contours of our heart."
~ Jose Ortega y Gassett
On Love: Aspects of a Single Theme

July 10th *I'll Close My Eyes – Dinah Washington*
"Although I conquer all the earth,
yet for me there is only one city.
In that city there is for me only one house;
And in that house, one room only;
And in that room, a bed.
And one woman sleeps there,
The shining joy and jewel of all my kingdom."
~ "Poems from the Sanscrit"
translated by John Brough

July 11th *My One & Only Love – Johnny Hartman*
"God is challenging you to find within your dating
'vertical' renewal rather than 'horizontal' renewal…
God teaches us that the deepest type of fulfillment and
the greatest new discoveries come about vertically, by
looking down into our own souls rather than across to a
new partner. If we reach deeper within the same
relationship, into the recesses of our own and our
partner's soul, we will come upon amazing new
discoveries and richness. You have to learn to tap into
this – the spring of new life inside yourself. Love is
infinite and we must plumb its depths. Those who do
obtain the deepest experience and understanding of this
life's greatest blessing and treasure, whereas those who
do not never attain more than a superficial knowledge

of it."
  ~ Rabbi Shmuley Boteach
  Dating Secrets of the Ten Commandments

July 12th *I Got Lost In His Arms – Shirley Horn*
"Thus love is the most universal experience of grace among human beings. Through all the ages men have sung in poetry and written in drama this curious fact: that sexual love has the power to take one out of the prison of oneself, to give one a greater life in exchange for the narrow one one loses, and to bring a quality of happiness that is, indeed, a 'little bit of heaven'…Such a relationship furnishes a peace and stability which are integral parts of lasting human happiness. It gives a sense of being 'at home' in the universe which relieves one of many vague and floating anxieties."
  ~ Rollo May, *The Springs of Creative Living*

July 13th *Heart & Soul – Helen Ward*
"Charms strike the sight,
But merit wins the soul."
  ~ Alexander Pope, "Rape of the Lock"

July 14th *Soul On Fire – Lavern Baker*
"The Mysterious Hidden Woman loves privacy, overhanging trees, long skirts, the shadowy places underneath bridges, rooms with low lighting. One intense sexual storm in a hay barn means more to her than three years of tepid lovemaking; she wants passion and purpose in a man, and carries a weighty desire in

her, a passion somewhere between erotic feeling and religious intensity."

~ Robert Bly, *Iron John*

July 15th *I've Got You Under My Skin — Dinah Washington*
"My desire for you is not trivial; I can compare it with the greatest of those accidents. But the energy it draws on might lead to racing a cold engine, cracking the frozen spiderweb, parachuting into the field of a poem wired with danger, or a trip through gorges and canyons, into the cratered night of female memory, where delicately and with intense care the chieftainess inscribes upon the ribs of the volcano the name of the one she has chosen."

~ Adrienne Rich, "Re-Forming the Crystal"

July 16th *Singing In The Rain — Lena Horne*
"The lips of the one I love are my perpetual pleasure:
The Lord be praised; for my heart's desire is attained."

~ Hafiz, "The Lord Be Praised"

July 17th *The Best Is Yet To Come — Frank Sinatra*
"Grow old along with me!
The best is yet to be,
The last of life, for which the first was made:
Our times are in his hand
Who saith 'a whole I planned,
Youth shows but half: trust God: see all
not be afraid!'"

~ Robert Browning, "Rabbi Ben Ezra"

July 18th *Our Love Is Here To Stay – Louis Armstrong &*
Ella Fitzgerald

"The specter of binding ourselves to cherish and care for a friend, a child, a lover, a mate, in an unknown future arouses our fears of being imprisoned within a space too small for our spirit…Entangling alliances may bind us too closely for comfort, but life without entwinement is a fragile as a rope of sand…To cobble together a life without commitments, a life of one-night stands, tentative relationships, and limited engagements is a guarantee of superficiality and loneliness…The pledge that we will cherish those we have chosen to love for better or worse…is the consequence of having accepted the love bond as something that needs fierce protection, because without it our lives would have no continuity, no depth, and no bulwark against the fickleness of circumstances. An irrevocable promise is the precondition for whole-hearted passion. I cannot act with trust and abandon until I decide that I will place the whole momentum of my being at the disposal of my decision. I become a fully engaged person only when I betroth myself, promise fidelity, to my friend, my mate, my vocation, my place, my community."

~ Sam Keen, *To Love and Be Loved*

July 19th *For Once In My Life – Tony Bennett*
"Love gives us purpose… But the purpose is never an abstract plan, never a blueprint of universal reason… The wisdom of the love song tells us that the place we will find purpose and meaning is in what is

idiosyncratic, unique, individual, unrepeatable, fragile, personal, exceptional."
~ Sam Keen, *The Passionate Life*

July 20th *I'm Glad There Is You – Carmen McRae*
"*'Volo ut sis'* ~ I want you to be."   ~ St. Augustine

July 21st *I Concentrate On You – Dinah Washington*
"Love alone is capable of uniting living beings in such a way as to complete and fufill them, for it alone takes them and joins them by what is deepest within themselves."
~ Pierre Teilhard de Chardin, *The Phenomenon of Man*

July 22nd *Time After Time – Chet Baker*
"One can truly, seriously promise to love only to the extent that whether we love is under our control. But we can affect whether we love. Love is not just a feeling. Part of what it is to love someone is to treat that person a certain way. Doing that is wholly in our power…To love someone and to continue to do it requires a certain directing of our thoughts and attention. If I sit and think about my wife, it is up to me to decide what I think about…It is all up to me, and if I think negatively often enough, I won't have much of a marriage left. In promising to love my wife, I undertake to direct my very thoughts to that end – to dwell most on what is good in my wife and (as far as I can) think only charitably on the rest."
~ Brian Leftow, *God and the Philosophers*

July 23rd *First Time Ever I Saw Your Face – Roberta Flack*
"It was a quiet way
He asked if I was his.
I made no answer of the tongue
But answer of the eyes.
And then he bore me high…
The world did drop away…
Eternity it was- before
Eternity was due.
No seasons were to us-
It was not night or noon,
For sunrise stopped upon the place
And fastened it in dawn."
~ Emily Dickinson
"It was a Quiet Way"

July 24th *Evergreen – Barbra Streisand*
"Shallowness and superficiality are the scourges of marriage, destroying intimacy and passion by covering over the full color and magnetism of the human soul. This is why in strengthening our marriages and relationships, we must focus on enlivening our personalities and ennobling our character…We must begin to focus more on the depth of personality and assure that our deepest selves are at least as attractive as our outer body. In pursuit of this goal, spiritual values, shared between two loving adults, pulls a couple together with something wholesome and eternal."
~ Rabbi Shmuley Boteach, *Kosher Sex*

July 25ᵗʰ *Power Of Love – Celine Dion*
"They tried to speak but they could not. Tears stood in their eyes. They were both pale and thin, but in their white sick faces there glowed the dawn of a new future, a perfect resurrection into a new life. Love had raised them from the dead, and the heart of each held endless springs of life for the heart of the other."
  ~ Feodor Dostoevsky, *Crime and Punishment*

July 26ᵗʰ *I'll Stand By You – The Pretenders*
"The ground of a strong and lasting commitment is the passionate connection between two people whose beings say yes to each other. When two people connect being-to-being, they experience a deep 'soul-resonance' that goes beyond mere romance or desire. Something powerful and real inside them starts waking up and coming alive in each other's presence. It is often surprising because they cannot reason themselves into or out of it… Out of this passionate resonance grows a devotion to each other's unfolding – which can allow them to persevere through difficult times and overcome any obstacles that threaten to come between them."
  ~ John Welwood, *Journey of the Heart*

July 27ᵗʰ *By Your Side - Sade*
"In true marriage lies
Nor equal, nor unequal. Each fulfills
Defect in each, and always thought in thought,
Purpose in purpose, will in will, they grow,
The single pure and perfect animal,

The two-celled heart beating, with one full strike,
Life."
~ Alfred, Lord Tennyson
"The Princess: A Medley"

July 28th *All About Soul – Billy Joel*
"Perhaps love isn't the word for it. Something greater
than the personal opens, burns, and rises through. It
cannot be understood or described, but it can be lived.
There is a mystery called the glance, the gift, nazaar... I
don't think it matters whether one has a living teacher
or not, one can still live in the glance of the soul guide,
the inner friendship. A wonderful statement of that
enveloping vision is Rumi's line, 'I see my beauty in
you.' A spiritual alchemy takes place inside the glance.
Desire changes and becomes a continuous moment...
The realm of the glance is beyond touch and somehow
within touch too."
~ *Rumi: The Glance: Songs of Soul-Meeting*
translated by Coleman Barks

July 29th *You Decorated My Life – Kenny Rogers*
"Music I heard with you was more than music
And bread I broke with you was more than bread."
~ Conrad Aiken, "Music I Heard"

July 30th *Through the Years – Kenny Rogers*
"When I die, I want your hands on my eyes;
I want the light and the wheat of your beloved hands
to pass their freshness over me once more:

I want to feel the softness that changed my destiny."
  ~ Pablo Neruda, "Love Sonnet LXXXIX"

July 31ˢᵗ *As Time Goes By – Ella Fitzgerald*
"In that last while, eternity's confine,
I came to love, I came into my own."
  ~ Theodore Roethke, "The Dream"

AUGUST: HARMONY

August 1st *Aquarius/Let the Sunshine – 5th Dimension*
"If the New Age is to begin to offer anything substantial to the reordering of life on earth, we Peter Pans have to land on *terra firma* and begin the hard work of transformation – first in our own lives, then in the world in front of us here and now, not in some distant past or uncertain future. To paraphrase the Buddhist sage: 'Do you want to change the world? Then park your mountain bike, get a job and start sweeping the street in front of your door.'"
~ John Babbs, *Meeting the Shadow*

August 2nd *Generation (Light Up the Sky) – Rare Earth*
"The outcome of the world, the gates of the future, the entry into the super-human--these are not thrown open to a few of the privileged nor to one chosen people to the exclusion of all others. They will open only to an advance of all together, in a direction in which all together can join and find completion in a spiritual renovation of the earth."
~ Pierre Teilhard de Chardin
The Phenomenon of Man

August 3rd *Draggin' The Line – Tommy James*
"Sometimes as I drift idly on Walden Pond, I cease to live and begin to be."
~ Henry David Thoreau, *Walden*

August 4ᵗʰ *Crystal Blue Persuasion – Tommy James*
"But lulled into such an opium-like listlessness of vacant, unconscious reverie is this absent-minded youth by the blending cadence of waves with thoughts, that at last he loses his identity; takes the mystic ocean at this feet for the visible image of that deep, blue, bottomless soul, pervading mankind and nature; and every strange, half-seen, gliding, beautiful thing that eludes him; every dimly discovered, uprising fin of some indiscernible form, seems to him the embodiment of those elusive thoughts that only people the soul by continually flitting through it. In this enchanted mood, thy spirit ebbs away to whence it came; becomes diffused through time and space; like Wickliffe's sprinkled Pantheistic ashes, forming at last a part of every shore the round globe over."
~ Herman Melville, *Moby Dick*

August 5ᵗʰ *Within You, Without You – George Harrison*
"Study yourself with unswerving attention, put aside all that is not self, proceed with the sense ever more closely directed to the purely inward. The more you pass by all foreign elements, making your personality appear diminished almost to the vanishing point, the clearer the Universe stands before you, and the more gloriously the terror of annihilating the fleeting is rewarded by the feeling of the feeling of the eternal… Soon everything individual and distinct will have been lost and the Universe will be found."
~ Friedrich Schleiermacher, *On Religion*

August 6th *Hurdy Gurdy - Donovan*

"Your inner Reality, your innermost Consciousness, which is constantly watching the mind, is different from the mind. Let the mind think whatever it likes. At the same time be aware that you are not the mind, you are only the witness of the mind; you are the observer, the spectator, who is watching the mind move. Knowledge is another name for right understanding of the mind. When our mind becomes agitated or turbulent, we should not think that we have become agitated or turbulent. We should be able to watch our turbulence or our agitation from a distance and see the endless creations of the mind."

~ Muktananda

August 7th *New World Coming – Mama Cass Elliot*

"To-day's situation is an historical emergence: it too will pass, unless we bungle our intellectual synthesizing task. Planetary intellectual cohesion need be attained in principle only once. No doubt it will be a pluralistic unity, in which the rich diversity of cultural and ideational forms will be understood by intelligent men and women everywhere within a comprehensive intellectual context that makes coherent sense of that very diversity. It happens to fall to our lot in contemporary history to construct that intellectual context."

~ Wilfred Cantrell Smith
Faith & Belief

August 8th *I Have a Dream – Solomon Burke*
"I have a dream today…when we let freedom ring, when we let it ring from every village and every hamlet, from every state and every city, we will be able to speed up that day when all of God's children, black men and white men, Jews and Gentiles, Protestants and Catholics, will be able to join hands and sing in the words of the old Negro spiritual, 'Free at last! Free at last! Thank God Almighty, we are free at last.'"
  ~ Martin Luther King, Jr., *Letter from Birmingham Jail*

August 9th *I'd Like to Teach the World to Sing-New Seekers*
"The shut-up person lacks communicativeness, whereas 'freedom,' Kierkegaard wrote, 'is continually communicating.' Thus the concentric circles of the widening and the deepening self involve at the same time the expanding circles of meaningful relations with one's fellowmen. He believed the two sources of neurotic anxiety – disunity within the self and lack of accord with one's fellows – are overcome by simultaneous processes; to overcome one is to overcome the other at the same time."
  ~ Rollo May, *Psychology and the Human Dilemma*

August 10th *What the World Needs Now-Jackie DeShannon*
"Love is not primarily a relationship to a specific person; it is an attitude, an ordination of character which determines the relatedness of the person to the whole world as a whole, not toward an object of love."
  ~ Eric Fromm, *The Art of Loving*

August 11th *All You Need is Love – The Beatles*
"Blessed is the influence of one true, loving human soul on another."
~ George Eliot, *Janet's Repentance*

August 12th *Put a Little Love in Your Heart - Jackie DeShannon*
"It is easier to love humanity than to love one's neighbor."
~ Eric Hoffer
The Ordeal of Change

August 13th *Give Me Love – George Harrison*
"Love hinders death. Love is life. All, everything that I understand, I understand only because I love. Everything is, everything exists, only because I love. Everything is united by it alone. Love is God, and to die means that I, a particle of love, shall return to the general and eternal source."
~ Leo Tolstoy, *War and Peace*

August 14th *Let Love Rule – Lenny Kravitz*
"Was he afraid or tranquil?
Might he know
How conscious consciousness could grow,
Till love that was, and love too blest to be
Meet – and the junction be Eternity?"
~ Emily Dickinson
"To know just how he suffered would be dear"

August 15th *Love Train – The O' Jays*

"Forgiving love is a possibility only for those who know that they are not good, who feel themselves in need of divine mercy, who live in a dimension deeper and higher than that of moral idealism…When life is lived in this dimension, the chasms which divide men are bridged not directly, not by resolving the conflicts on the historical levels, but by the sense of an ultimate unity in, and common dependence on, the realm of transcendence. For this reason the religious ideal of forgiveness is more profound and more difficult than the rational virtue of tolerance."

~ Reinhold Niebuhr, *An Interpretation of Christian Ethics*

August 16th *United We Stand – Brotherhood of Man*

"United we stand, divided we fall."

~ Aesop, "The Four Oxen & the Lion" *Fables*

August 17th *He Ain't Heavy, He's My Brother – The Hollies*

"There is a destiny that makes us brothers,
none goes his way alone.
All that we send into the lives of others
comes back into our own."

~ Edwin Markham, "A Creed"

August 18th *Share the Land – The Guess Who*

"We cannot know whether we love God, although there may be strong reason for thinking so; but there can be no doubt about whether we love our neighbor or not. Be sure that, in proportion as you advance in fraternal

charity, you are increasing your love of God."
~ St. Teresa of Avila, *The Interior Castle*

August 19th *Let's Work Together — Canned Heat*
"There is neither East nor West, Border, nor Breed, nor Birth, / When two strong men stand face to face, though they come from the ends of the earth."
~ Rubyard Kipling, "The Ballad of East and West"

August 20th *Put Your Hands Together — The O' Jays*
"Then let us pray that come it may,
As come it will for a' that,
That sense and worth, o'er a' the earth,
May bear the gree [victory], an a' that,
For a' that, an' a' that,
It's coming yet, for a' that,
That man to man, the world o'er,
Shall brothers be for a' that."
~ Robert Burns, "A Man's a Man for a' That"

August 21st *Friendship Train — Gladys Knight*
"A friend is one to whom one may pour out all the contents of one's heart, chaff and grain together, knowing that the gentlest of hands will take and sift it, keep what is worth keeping and with the breath of kindness blow the rest away."
~ Arabian proverb

August 22nd *The Onion Song — Marvin Gaye*
"The good neighbor looks beyond the external

accidents and discerns those inner qualities that make all men human, and, therefore, brothers."

~ Martin Luther King, Jr., *Strength to Love*

August 23rd *Everyday People – Sly & the Family Stone*
"If we meet no gods it is because we harbor none. If there is grandeur in you, you will find grandeur in porters and in sweeps."

~ Ralph Waldo Emerson, *The Conduct of Life*

August 24th *Love, Peace & Happiness – Chamber Brothers*
"The more a person becomes mature, the more he comes to recognize, and turn to a truly personal conviction, that his own individual good is joined inseparably with the good of other persons in ever-widening circles until his horizon of judgment finally takes in the entire human race as one and indivisible in interdependence, destiny, and happiness... Existentially this is a wisdom gained by experience and good living. Philosophically it is rooted in the very nature of the person as a self whose very self-hood is intrinsically constituted in relation to other selves."

~ W. Norris Clarke
Conscience: Its Freedom and Limitations

August 25th *We've Got To Have Peace – Curtis Mayfield*
"We must learn to live together as brothers or perish together as fools."

~ Martin Luther King, Jr.
Speech at St. Louis, March 22, 1964

August 26th *Give Peace a Chance – John Lennon*

"At the center of nonviolence stands the principle of love. The nonviolent resister would contend that in the struggle for human dignity, the oppressed people of the world must not succumb to the temptation of becoming bitter or indulging in hate campaigns. To retaliate in kind would do nothing but intensify the existence of hate in the universe. Along the way of life, someone must have sense enough and morality enough to cut off the chain of hate. This can only be done by projecting the ethic of love to the center of our lives."

~ Martin Luther King, Jr., *Stride Toward Freedom*

August 27th *Peace Train – Cat Stevens*

"The test is simple: if people's beliefs -- secular or religious -- make them belligerent, intolerant, and unkind about other people's faith, they are not 'skillful.' If, however, their convictions impel them to act compassionately and to honor the stranger, then they are good, helpful, and sound. This is the test of true religiosity."

~ Karen Armstrong, *The Great Transformation*

August 28th *Let There Be Peace On Earth – Gladys Knight*

"Lord, make me an instrument of your peace;
where there is hatred, let me sow love;
when there is injury, pardon;
where there is doubt, faith;
where there is despair, hope;
where there is darkness, light;

and where there is sadness, joy.
Grant that I may not so much seek
to be consoled as to console;
to be understood, as to understand,
to be loved as to love;
for it is in giving that we receive,
it is in pardoning that we are pardoned,
and it is in dying [to ourselves] that we are born to
eternal life."
  ~ Peace Prayer attributed to St. Francis of Assisi

August 29th *Get Together – The Youngbloods*
"No man is an island entire of itself;
every man is part of the main…
Any man's death diminishes me because
I am involved in mankind,
And therefore never send to know
for whom the bell tolls;
It tolls for thee."
  ~ John Donne, "Meditation XVII"

August 30th *One Love – Bob Marley*
"The deepest level of communication is not communication, but communion. It is wordless. It is beyond words, and it is beyond speech, and it is beyond concept. Not that we discover a new unity. We discover an older unity. My dear Brothers [and Sisters], we are already one. But we imagine that we are not. And what we have to recover is our original unity. What we have to be is what we are."

~ Thomas Merton, *Choosing to Love the World*

August 31st *Reach Out Of Darkness – Friends of Distinction*
"The dialogical person is a related person. By this we mean that he responds to others and is, therefore, responsible…The dialogical word is an open word, a word of beginnings, because it is a word of expectation inviting response. In speaking the word of dialogue a person puts himself on the threshold of truth and becomes the servant of God."
~ Reuel L. Howe, *The Miracle of Dialogue*

SEPTEMBER: ETHICS

September 1ˢᵗ *Blowing in the Wind – Johnny Cash*
"Everyone says forgiveness is a lovely idea, until they have something to forgive, as we had during the war. And then, to mention the subject at all is to be greeted with howls of anger... I am not trying to tell you in this book what I could do — I can do precious little — I am telling you Christianity is. I did not invent it. And there, right in the middle of it, I find 'Forgive us our sins as we forgive those that sin against us.'"
~ C.S. Lewis, *Mere Christianity*

September 2ⁿᵈ *Which Way Are You Going? – Jim Croce*
"You cannot play with the animal in you without becoming wholly animal, play with falsehood without forfeiting your right to truth, play with cruelty without losing your sensitivity of mind. He who wants to keep his garden tidy doesn't reserve a plot for weeds."
~ Dag Hammarskjold, *Markings*

September 3ʳᵈ *You've Got to Stand for Something – Aaron Tippin*
"Ultimate concern perhaps is the concept closest to what we mean by a moral purpose. Named by theologian Paul Tillich, ultimate concern refers to whatever we make the central concern of our lives... From a theological perspective, Tillich suggests it is idolatrous for us to make an object of ultimate concern anything that is not truly ultimate... Standing for

something is the quality of ultimate concern. We stand for those things to which we are ultimately committed and from which we derive our ultimate fulfillment."
~ Douglas V. Porpora, *Landscapes of the Soul*

September 4th *I Wonder What Would Happen To This World – Harry Chapin*
"Life energy is all we have. It is precious because it is limited and irretrievable and because our choices about how we use it express the meaning and purpose of our time here on earth."
~ Joe Dominguez & Vicki Robin
Your Money or Your Life

September 5th *If I Can Dream – Elvis Presley*
"Let us not wallow in the valley of despair. I say to you today, my friends, that in spite of the difficulties and frustrations of the moment, I still have a dream. It is a dream deeply rooted in the American dream. I have a dream that one day this nation will rise up and live out the true meaning of its creed: 'We hold these truths to be self-evident: that all men are created equal.'"
~ Martin Luther King, Jr., "I Have a Dream"

September 6th *If I Had a Hammer - Peter, Paul & Mary*
"Action springs not from thought, but from a readiness for responsibility."
~ Dietrich Bonhoeffer
Letters and Papers from Prison

September 7ᵗʰ *If You're Ready – The Staple Singers*
"The encounter with God does not come to man in order that he many henceforth attend to God, but in order that he may prove its meaning in action in the world."
~ Martin Buber, *I and Thou*

September 8ᵗʰ *Stand – Sly & the Family Stone*
"Cowards can never be moral."
~ Mahatma Gandhi

September 9ᵗʰ *Get Up, Stand Up – Bob Marley*
"The dispassionate, postmodern, cool man is the antithesis of the phallic male – no passion, no standing forth, no risk, no eros, no drive to survive and enrich history. Nor is the 'new age' man who is self-absorbed in his own feelings and committed to 'personal growth' a candidate for heroism… Our loss has been ontological, not psychological. A deficiency in meaning and in being. A refusal to care for what matters, a limpness in the face of the challenge of our history. The challenges seem overwhelming, and we are understandably tempted to retreat into professions and corporations that swallow us, into private pleasures and high consumption. But let's call that what it is: moral cowardice, abdication of responsibility, voluntary myopia. And if we continue on this path we will continue to feel empty and devoid of meaning."
~ Sam Keen, *Fire in the Belly*

September 10th *Ball of Confusion – The Temptations*
"The dignity that I have observed has to do with the harmony of commitment, knowledge, and work. Commitment involves a clear sense of what a person is devoted to, how one believes a life should be lived. The simplest way to indignity is the acquiescent confusion that draws the current creed from the day's broadcast signals. A person with this uncritical receptivity can hardly even be present to another; when we cannot sense another's orienting commitments, we begin to suspect that we are not talking to anyone at all"
~ Jedediah Purdy
For Common Things

September 11th *Abraham, Martin & John – Marvin Gaye*
"The ultimate weakness of violence is that it is a descending spiral, begetting the very thing it seeks to destroy. Instead of diminishing evil, it multiplies it. Through violence you may murder the liar, but you cannot murder the lie, nor establish the truth. Through violence you may murder the hater, but you do not murder hate. In fact, violence merely increases hate. So it goes. ... Returning hate for hate multiplies hate, adding deeper darkness to a night already devoid of stars. Darkness cannot drive out darkness: only light can do that. Hate cannot drive out hate: only love can do that."
~ Martin Luther King, Jr.,
"Where Do We Go From Here?"

September 12th *Keep On Keeping On – Curtis Mayfield*

"I accept this award today with an abiding faith in America and an audacious faith in the future of mankind. I refuse to accept despair as the final response to the ambiguities of history. I refuse to accept the idea that the 'isness' of man's present nature makes him morally incapable of reaching up for the eternal 'oughtness' that forever confronts him. I refuse to accept the idea that man is mere flotsam and jetsam in the river of life, unable to influence the unfolding events which surround him. I refuse to accept the view that mankind is so tragically bound to the starless midnight of racism and war that the bright daybreak of peace and brotherhood can never become a reality. I refuse to accept the cynical notion that nation after nation must spiral down a militaristic stairway into the hell of thermonuclear destruction. I believe that unarmed truth and unconditional love will have the final word in reality. This is why right, temporarily defeated, is stronger than evil triumphant."

~ Martin Luther King, Jr.
Nobel Prize acceptance speech (1964)

September 13th *Now – Lena Horne*

"Now is the accepted time, not tomorrow, not some more convenient season. It is today that our best work can be done and not some future day or future year. It is today that we fit ourselves for the greater usefulness of tomorrow. Today is the seed time, now are the hours of work, and tomorrow comes the harvest and the playtime." ~ W. E. B. Du Bois

September 14th *Eyes On The Prize – Mavis Staples*
"We've got some difficult days ahead. But it really doesn't matter with me now, because I've been to the mountaintop. And I don't mind. Like anybody, I would like to live along life. Longevity has its place. But I'm not concerned about that now. I just want to do God's will. And He's allowed me to go to the mountain, and I've looked over, and I've seen the promised land. I may not get there with you. But I want you to know tonight that we, as a people, will get to the promised land. And I'm so happy tonight. I'm not worried about anything. I'm not fearing any man. Mine eyes have seen the glory of the coming of the Lord."
  ~ Martin Luther King, Jr.
  Speech on 4-3-68 in Memphis, TN

September 15th *Freedom Highway – Staple Singers*
"When great causes are on the move in the world, stirring all men's souls, drawing them from their firesides, casting aside comfort, wealth, and the pursuit of happiness in response to impulses at once awe-striking and irresistible, we learn that we are spirits not animals."
  ~ Winston Churchill, radio broadcast 6-16-41

September 16th *In My Own Lifetime – Sammy Davis, Jr.*
"Let America be America again.
Let it be the dream it used to be.

Let America be the dream the dreamers dreamed —
Let it be that great strong land of love
Where never kings connive nor tyrants scheme
That any man be crushed by one above.
O, let my land be a land where Liberty
Is crowned with no false patriotic wreath,
But opportunity is real, and life is free,
Equality is in the air we breathe."
   ~ Langston Hughes, "A New Song"

September 17th *Dialogue - Chicago*
"One has to expose oneself – and those whom one
wants to persuade rationally of the merits of one's own
position – to objections and replies and to encounters
with alternatives… A man who does not consider how
his actions are likely to affect other people is to that
extent irresponsible, even if he acts on 'principle' …To
be responsible and rational in such matters, one must
consider what can be said against one's moral principles
and standards. The man who gives no thought to
objections and alternatives is, to that extent, irrational.
But if one considers the codes of different religions and
societies, the arguments of outstanding philosophers,
relevant plays and novels, and concrete situations as
well, moral judgments based on such reflection are, to
that extent, informed, responsible, and rational."
   ~ Walter Kaufman, *The Faith of a Heretic*

September 18th *She Is Always Seventeen – Harry Chapin*
"By demonstrating that certain ways of living are

possible, they invite others to live in the same ways…These people present us with moral arguments articulated in flesh and effort. Often, only knowing them can make it possible to speak confidently of the ideals that they enact. If we do not encounter such lives, the ideals may become unspeakable as well."

~ Jedediah Purdy, *For Common Things*

September 19th *Fly Like an Eagle – Steve Miller Band*
"Each time a man stands up for an ideal, or acts to improve the lot of others, or strikes out against injustice, he sends forth a tiny ripple of hope… and crossing each other from a million different centers of energy and daring those ripples build a current that can sweep down the mightiest walls of oppression and resistance."

~ Robert Kennedy
"Speech at University of Capetown," 6/6/1966

September 20th *Give a Little Bit - Supertramp*
"I shall pass through this world but once, any good therefore that I can do or any kindness I can show to any human being, let me do it now… for I shall not pass this way again."

~ Etienne de Giellet

September 21st *We Are The World – USA for Africa*
"My country is the world, and my religion is to do good."

~ Thomas Paine, *Rights of Man*

September 22nd *None of Us Are Free – Solomon Burke*

"It seems to me, in reflecting upon the progress of moral thinking down the ages, especially on those moments when the moral wisdom of a society evolves decisively and reverses or notably qualifies previously held moral principles, that what usually happens is that a wider context of reality with new relevant consequences comes into focus, or that it becomes recognized that the previous judgments were made from too narrow a value perspective, subordinating a higher but less apparent value to a more immediately evident shorter-range one."

~ W. Norris Clarke
Conscience: Its Freedom and Limitations

September 23rd *Rockin' in the Free World – Neil Young*

"The capitalist order is now global in extent. It is a reign not of God but of desire. It has been called McWorld. McWorld is the reign of corporate power... Seduced into civic mindlessness, we accept what we are served... This is a profound alienation... The religions of the East have a word for our condition. They call it avidya. Avidya is such fascination with the superficialities of life that we fail to turn our attention to anything higher or deeper... McWorld is not the image to offer back to the Absolute Spirit. Our call is to fashion a world order that is."

~ Douglas V. Porpora, *Landscapes of the Soul*

September 24th *Land Of Confusion - Genesis*

"'Learning what is true in order to do what is right' is

the summing up of the whole duty of man."
~ Thomas H. Huxley
Lay Sermons, Addresses and Reviews

September 25th *The Way It Is – Bruce Hornsby & Tupac*
"You do not take a person who for years has been hobbled by chains and liberate him, bringing him up to the starting line of a race and then say, 'You are free to compete with all of the others,' and still justly believe that you have been completely fair… It is not enough just to open the gates of opportunity. All of our citizens must have the ability to walk through those gates."
~ Lyndon Johnson
Commencement Address at Howard University

September 26th *Another Day in Paradise – Phil Collins*
"Put in simple terms, piety means the deep down recognition of our frailty and dependence, the acknowledgment that the burden we inherit cannot be sustained unaided, the disposition to give thanks for our existence and reverence for the world on which we depend, and the sense of unfathomable mystery which surrounds our coming to be and our passing away."
~ Roger Scruton
An Intelligent Person's Guide to Philosophy

September 27th *What's Up – 4 Non Blondes*
"Is This the Thing the Lord God made and gave
To have dominion over sea and land;
To trace the stars and search the heavens for power;

To feel the passion of eternity?
Is this the dream He dreamed who shaped the suns
And marked their ways upon the ancient deep?
Down all the caverns of Hell to their last gulf
There is no shape more terrible than this –
More tongued with censure of the world's blind greed –
More filled with sighs and portents for the soul –
More packt with danger for the universe.
What gulfs between him and the seraphim!
Slave of the wheel of labor, what to him
Are Plato and the swing of Pleiades?…
O masters, lords, and rulers in all lands,
Is this the handiwork you give to God?"
    ~ Edwin Markham, "The Man with the Hoe"

September 28th *Man in the Mirror – Michael Jackson*
"Let him that would move the world, first move himself."
    ~ Socrates

September 29th *I Have a Dream – Common*
"Hold fast to dreams
For if dreams die
Life is a broken-winged bird
That cannot fly."
    ~ Langston Hughes, "Dreams"

September 30th *Higher Ground – Stevie Wonder*
"Ideals are like stars; you will not succeed in touching them with your hands, but like the seafaring man on the

desert of waters, you choose them as your guides, and following them you reach your destiny."

~ Carl Schurz

"True Americanism" *Speeches of Carl Schurz*

OCTOBER: WISDOM

October 1ˢᵗ *What a Wonderful World – Louis Armstrong*
"Thanks to the human heart by which we live,
Thanks to its tenderness, its joys, and fears,
To me the meanest flower that blows can give
Thoughts that do often lie too deep for tears."
~ William Wordsworth
"Ode of Intimations of Immortality"

October 2ⁿᵈ *I've Got the Sun in the Morning – Barbara Cook*
"To live content with small means; to seek elegance rather than luxury, and refinement rather than fashion; to be worthy, not respectable, and wealthy, not rich; to study hard, think quietly, talk gently, act frankly; to listen to the stars and birds, to babes and sages, with open heart; to bear all cheerfully, do all bravely, await occasions, hurry never. In a word, to let the spiritual, unbidden, and unconscious, grow up through the common. This is to be my symphony."
~ William Henry Channing, *My Symphony*

October 3ʳᵈ *I Got Plenty Of Nothin' – Frank Sinatra*
"A man is rich in proportion of the number of things he can afford to let alone."
~ Henry David Thoreau
"Where I Lived and What I Lived For"

October 4ᵗʰ *Give Me The Simple Life – June Christy*
"Since Transcendentalists were convinced that life was

too precious to waste on the mere pursuit and enjoyment of things, their common goal was to develop modes of living that reduced their material and institutional needs to a minimum so that they could more easily pursue spiritual truths, moral ideals, and aesthetic impulses."

~ David E. Shi, *The Simple Life*

October 5th *Enjoy Yourself – Louis Prima*
"What is joy? We can say, as the dictionary does, that it is 'an exultation of the spirit, the beatitude of paradise.' We can say that, unlike the ephemeral state of happiness, it is a lasting value that nourishes and sustains the spirit as well as the body. Joy does not induce a craving for more, because it is enough."

~ Robert A. Johnson
Ecstasy: Understanding the Psychology of Joy

October 6th *Are You Having Any Fun – Tony Bennett*
"I conceive that the great part of the miseries of mankind are brought upon them by false estimates they have made of the values of things."

~ Benjamin Franklin

October 7th *You've Got To Have Heart – Peggy Lee*
"Educating the mind without educating the heart is no education at all."   ~ Aristotle

October 8th *That's Life – Frank Sinatra*
"Men must endure

Their going hence, even as their coming hither:
Ripeness is all."
~ William Shakespeare, *King Lear*

October 9th *Be Thankful for What You've Got – William DeVaughn*
"Despite the popular notion that Stoicism means gritting your teeth in the face of discomfort – taking thins 'philosophically,' as people commonly say – the central concept of Stoicism is to value only that which no one can take from you. Value, then, is found in things like virtue...For the Stoics, the goal is to maintain power over yourself. If you value something that can be taken away, you put yourself in the power of whoever can take it."
~ Lou Marinoff, *Plato Not Prozac!*

October 10th *Be What You Are – The Staple Singers*
"Rabbi Zusya said that on the Day of Judgment, God would ask him, not why he had not been Moses, but why he had not been Zusya."
~ Walter Kaufman,
The Faith of a Heretic

October 11th *God Bless the Child – Blood, Sweat & Tears*
"This above all; to thine own self be true,
And it must follow, as the night the day,
Thou canst not then be false to any man."
~ William Shakespeare, *Hamlet*

October 12th *I Got a Name — Jim Croce*

"Never esteem anything as of advantage to you that will make you break your word or lose your self-respect."
~ Marcus Aurelius Antoninus, *Meditations*

October 13th *Garden Party — Rick Nelson*

"Hard is his lot that, here by fortune placed,
Much watch the wild vicissitudes of taste;
With every meteor of caprice must play,
And chase the new-blown bubbles of the day.
Ah! Let not censure term our fate our choice,
The stage but echoes back the public voice:
The drama's laws, the drama's patrons give,
For we that live to please, must please to live."
~ Samuel Johnson
"Prologue Spoken by Mr. Garrick"

October 14th *Games People Play — Joe South*

"Fanaticism is always a sign that one has adopted one of a pair of opposites at the expense of the other. The high energy of fanaticism is a frantic effort to keep one half of the truth at bay while the other half takes control. This always yields a brittle and unrelatable personality."
~ Robert A. Johnson, *Owning Your Own Shadow*

October 15th *Mind Games — John Lennon*

"Now I am suggesting that maintaining the tension between seeming 'opposites' is the chief way to cope with most of our dilemmas in the modern world. And this is just about the hardest attitude imaginable for a

race of beings conditioned for millennia to swing to one opposite or the other, to view life as an immutable dualism between the 'good' (my way) and the 'bad' (your way)... Adopting a middle-of-the-road position is usually just tepidity and timidity, but to grasp a paradox and to hold it in tension, requires courage and wisdom... Holding the polarities in tension means finding the optimum point at which they work together best; and this is not necessarily the middle."
  ~ Sydney J. Harris, *The Authentic Person*

October 16th *Watching The Wheels – John Lennon*
"Fast is busy, controlling, aggressive, hurried, analytical, stressed, superficial, inpatient, active, quantity-over-quality. Slow is the opposite: calm, careful, receptive, still, intuitive, unhurried, patient, reflective, quality-over-quantity. It is about making real and meaningful connections – with people, culture, work, food, everything."
  ~ Carl Honore, *In Praise of Slowness*

October 17th *Let It Be – The Beatles*
"But the love towards a thing infinite and eternal alone feeds the mind with a pleasure secure from all pain...The greatest good is the knowledge of the union which the mind has with the whole of nature...The more the mind knows, the better it understands its forces or strengths, the better it will be able to direct itself and lay down the rules for itself; and the more it understands the order of nature, the more easily it will

be able to liberate itself from useless things; this is the whole method."

~ Baruch Spinoza
Improvement of the Intellect

October 18th *No Rain – Blind Melon*
"To see a World in a grain of sand,
And Heaven in a wild flower,
Hold Infinity in the palm of your hand,
And Eternity in an hour."

~ William Blake, "Auguries of Innocence"

October 19th *Time – Pink Floyd*
"I believe that the mind can be permanently profaned by the habit of attending to trivial things...
Read not the Times
Read the Eternities."

~ Henry David Thoreau, *Life Without Principle*

October 20th *Mahogany – Diana Ross*
"Fulfillment of your larger purpose may lie in the future, but the practices that get you there happen today...
Purpose, like meaning, often appears retroactively."

~ Lou Marinoff, *Plato Not Prozac!*

October 21st *What I Did For Love – A Chorus Line*
"For all the sad words of tongue or pen,
The saddest are these: 'It might have been!'"

~ John Greenleaf Whittier, "Maud Muller"

October 22ⁿᵈ *The Rose – Bette Midler*

"Every day I live I am more convinced that the waste of life lies in the love we have not given, the powers we have not used, the selfish prudence that will risk nothing and which, shirking pain, misses happiness as well."

~ Mary Cholmondeley

October 23ʳᵈ *Throw It Away – Abbey Lincoln*

"I think we can safely trust a good deal more than we do. We may waive just so much care of ourselves as we honestly bestow elsewhere."

~ Henry David Thoreau, *Walden*

October 24ᵗʰ *You Learn – Alanis Morissette*

"I have learned that success is to be measured not so much by the position that one has reached in life as by the obstacles which he has overcome while trying to succeed."

~ Booker T. Washington, *Up From Slavery*

October 25ᵗʰ *Live & Learn – Joe Public*

"Suppose a man can convince me of error and bring home to me that I am mistaken in thought or act; I shall be glad to alter, for the truth is what I pursue, and no one was ever injured by the truth, whereas he is injured who continues in his own self-deception and ignorance."

~ Marcus Aurelius Antoninus
Humanist Anthology: From Confucius to Bertrand Russell

October 26ᵗʰ *Life Is What You Make It – Talk Talk*
"Life is a selection, no more. The work of the gardener is simply to destroy this weed, or that shrub, or that tree, and leave this other to grow. The library is gradually made inestimable by taking out from the superabounding mass of books all but the best. The palace is a selection of materials; its architecture, a selection of the best effects. Things collect very fast of themselves; the difference between house and house is the wise omissions."
  ~ Ralph Waldo Emerson, *Journals*, 1846

October 27ᵗʰ *Choices – George Jones*
"We who had lived in the concentration camps can remember the men who walked through the huts comforting others, giving away their last piece of bread. They may have been few in number, but they offer sufficient proof that everything can be taken away from a man but one thing: the last of the human freedoms – to choose one's attitude in any given set of circumstances, to choose one's own way."
  ~ Viktor Frankl
  Man's Search for Meaning

October 28ᵗʰ *The Gambler – Kenny Rogers*
"We cannot withdraw our cards from the game. Were we as silent and as mute as stones, our very passivity would be an act."
  ~ Jean-Paul Sartre, *Situations*

October 29th *Simple Man – Lynryd Skynyrd*

"I went to the woods because I wished to live deliberately, to front only the essential facts of life, and see if I could not learn what it had to teach, and not when I came to die, discover that I had not lived. I did not wish to live what was not life, living is so dear; nor did I wish to practice resignation, unless it was quite necessary. I wanted to live deep and suck out the marrow of life, to live so sturdily and Spartan-like as to put to rout all that was not life, to cut a broad swath and shave close, to drive life into a corner, and reduce it to its lowest terms, and, if it proved to be mean, why then to get the whole and genuine meanness of it, and publish its meanness to the world; or if it were sublime, to know it by experience, and be able to give a true account of it in my next excursion."

~ Henry David Thoreau, *Walden*

October 30th *I Hope You Dance – Gladys Knight*

"It is not the not the critic who counts, not the man who points out how the strong man stumbled, or where the doer of deeds could have done better. The credit belongs to the man who is actually in the arena… who at best knows great achievement and who at the worst if he fails at least fails while daring greatly so that his place shall never be with those cold and timid souls who know neither victory nor defeat."

~ Theodore Roosevelt
1910 Speech @ Sorbonne, Paris

October 31st *Being Me – Abbey Lincoln*

"O me! O life! of the questions of these recurring, / Of the endless trains of the faithless, of cities fill'd with the foolish, / Of myself forever reproaching myself, (for who more foolish than I, / and who more faithless?) / Of eyes that vainly crave the light, of the objects mean, of the / struggle ever renew'd, / Of the poor results of all, of the plodding and sordid crowds I see / around me, / Of the empty and useless years of the rest, with the rest me intertwined, / The question, O me! so sad, recurring--What good amid these, O me, O life? / Answer. / That you are here--that life exists and identity, / That the powerful play goes on, and you may contribute a verse."

~ Walt Whitman, "O Me! O Life!"

NOVEMBER: REFLECTION

November 1ˢᵗ *I'm Still Here – Eartha Kitt*
"I stepped from plank to plank
A slow and cautious way/
The Stars about my Head I felt
About my Feet the Sea./ I knew not but the next
Would be my final inch –
This gave me that precarious Gait
Some call experience."
~ Emily Dickinson, "I Stepped from Plank to Plank"

November 2ⁿᵈ *Wasted on the Way – Crosby, Stills & Nash*
"The tragedy of life is what dies inside a man while he lives."
~ Albert Schweitzer

November 3ʳᵈ *I've Loved These Days – Billy Joel*
"If I were to begin life again, I should want it as it was. I would only open my eyes a little more."
~ Jules Renard, *Journal*, March 1906

November 4ᵗʰ *Like A Rock – Bob Seger*
"Sixty years ago I knew everything; now I know nothing: Education is the progressive discovery of our own ignorance."
~ Will Durant

November 5ᵗʰ *Landslide – Stevie Nicks*
"Now no joy but lacks salt

That is not dashed with pain
And weariness and fault;
I crave the stain
Of tears, the aftermark
Of almost too much love,
The sweet of bitter bark
And burning clove.
When stiff and sore and scarred
I take away my hand
From leaning on it hard
In grass and sand,
The hurt is not enough:
I long for weight and strength
To feel the earth as rough
To all my length."
    ~ Robert Frost. "To Earthward"

November 6th *Souvenir – Billy Joel*
"As a fond mother, when the day is o'er,
Leads by the hand her little child to bed,
Half willing, half reluctant to be led,
And leave his broken playthings on the floor,
Still gazing at them through the open door,
Nor wholly reassured and comforted
By promises of others in their stead,
Which, though more splendid, may not please him more;
So nature deals with us, and takes away
Our playthings one by one, and by the hand
Leads us to rest so gently, that we go

Scarce knowing if we wish to go or stay,
Being too full of sleep to understand
How far the unknown transcends the what we know.
~ Henry Wadsworth Longfellow, "Nature"

November 7th *Times Of Your Life – Paul Anka*
"The soulful move is the move toward contemplating the source of things deeply rooted in eternity, the things that always are… When we touch that mystery, we're nourished in a profound way. If we're not touching the eternals – if we're not in touch with mythic stories, with ancient sites, with old family scrapbooks and heirlooms and deeply probing relationships - then we're lost. If all we're trying to do is keep up with change, I think we lose the momentum of our soul's journey. But once you touch an old story, a true mentor, or the mysterious powers of nature, somehow your soul is nourished and, by a movement that stills mystifies me, you find the courage to go on."
~ Phil Cousineau, *The Handbook for the Soul*

November 8th *Try To Remember – Ed Ames*
"But man as such inclines to self-forgetfulness. He must snatch himself out of it if he is not to lose himself to the world, to habits, to thoughtless banalities, to the beaten track.. Philosophy is the decision to awaken our primal source, to find our way back to ourselves by inner action… And to lead a philosophical life means to take seriously our experience of men, of happiness and hurt, of success and failure, of the obscure and the

confused,"
~ Karl Jaspers, *The Way to Wisdom*

November 9th *It Was A Very Good Year – Frank Sinatra*
"Love, with very young people, is a heartless business, we drink at that age from thirst or to get drunk; it is only later in life that we occupy ourselves with the individuality of our wine."
~ Isak Dinesen, *Seven Gothic Tales*

November 10th *September Of My Years – Frank Sinatra*
"Soul or heart or a deep connectedness is always present, but we are not always in touch with it. Nourishing the soul is the process of drinking at the life stream, coming back to one's true self, embracing the whole of one's experience – good, bad, or ugly; painful or exalted; dull or boring… As you get older, a lifetime of not paying attention and not nourishing what is deepest and most important has profound consequences. The details and excitement of youth, work, ego gratification, the pursuit of name and fame, all fall away. What you're left with is the fundamentals you have been practicing… You get more and more locked into that behavior."
~ Jon Kabat-Zinn, *The Handbook for the Soul*

November 11th *September Song – Frank Sinatra*
"Some – perhaps most – human beings never know deep love until they experience, at someone's death, the preciousness of friendship, devotion, loyalty. Abraham

Maslow is profoundly right when he wonders whether we could love passionately if we knew we'd never die."
~ Rollo May, *Love and Will*

November 12ᵗʰ *When The World Was Young – Peggy Lee*
"Not for such hopes and fears
Annulling youth's brief years,
Do I remonstrate: folly wide the mark!
Rather I prize the doubt
Low kinds exist without,
Finished and finite clods, untroubled by a spark…
For thence, -- a paradox
Which comforts while it mocks,
Shall life succeed in that it seems to fail:
What I aspired to be, And was not, comforts me."
~ Robert Browning, "Rabbi Ben Ezra"

November 13ᵗʰ *Memory – Barbra Streisand*
"I think we are well advised to keep on nodding terms with the people we used to be, whether we find them attractive company or not. Otherwise they turn up unannounced and surprise us, come hammering on the mind's door at 4am of a bad night and demand to know who deserted them, who betrayed them, who is going to make amends. We forget all too soon the things we thought we could never forget. We forget the loves and the betrayals alike, forget what we whispered and what we screamed, forget who we were."
~ Joan Didion, "On Keeping a Notebook"
In Depth: Essays for our Time

November 14th *The Party Is Over – Shirley Bassey*

"The sun is folding, cars stall and rise / beyond the window. The workmen leave / the street to the bums and painters' wives / pushing their babies home. Those who realize / how fitful and indecent consciousness is/ Stare solemnly out on the empty street. / The mourners and soft singers: The liars, / and seekers after ridiculous righteousness. All / my doubles, and friends, whose mistakes cannot / be duplicated by machines, and this is all of our / arrogance. Being broke or broken, dribbling/ at the eyes. Wasted lyricists, and men / who have seen their dreams come true, only seconds / after they knew those dreams to be horrible conceits / and plastic fantasies of gesture and extension, / Shoulders, hair, and tongues distributing misinformation / about the nature of the understanding. No one is that simple/ or priggish, to be alone out of spite and grow strong / in its practice, mystics in two-pants suits. Our style, / and discipline, controlling the method of knowledge,/ Beatniks, like Bohemians, go calmly out of style / And boys / are dying in Mexico, who did not yet get the word. / The lateness of their fabrication: marks their holes / with filthy needles. The lust of the world. This will not / be news. The simple damning lust, / float flat magic in low changing / evenings. Shiver your hands / in dance. Empty all of me for / knowing, and will the danger / of identification, / Let me sit and go blind in my dreaming / and be that dream in purpose and device. / A fantasy of defeat, a strong strong man / older, but no wiser than the defect of love."

~ Amiri Baraka (aka Leroi Jones), "The New World"

November 15th *Those Were The Days – Mary Hopkins*
"For some we loved, the loveliest and the best
That from his Vintage rolling time hath prest,
Have drunk their Cup a Round or two before,
And one by one crept silently to rest…
Ah, make the most of what we yet may spend,
Before we too into the Dust descend;
Dust unto dust, and under Dust to lie,
Sans Wine, sans Song, sans Singer, and – sans End!"
   ~ Edward Fitzgerald
   "The Rubaiyat of Omar Khayyam"

November 16th *Days Of Wine & Roses – Tony Bennett*
"It is indeed from the experience of beauty and happiness, from the occasional harmony between our nature and our environment, that we can draw our conception of the divine life."
   ~ George Santayana, *The Sense of Beauty*

November 17th *Both Sides Now – Joni Mitchell*
"Insofar as the mind sees things in their eternal aspect, it participates in eternity."   ~ Baruch Spinoza, *Ethics*

November 18th *Truth, Bitter Truth – Marianne Faithfull*
"Give me truths;
For I am weary of surfaces,
And die of inanition."
   ~ Ralph Waldo Emerson, "Blight"

November 19th *Yesterdays – Billie Holiday*
"Though nothing can bring back the hour
Of splendor in the grass, of glory in the flower;
We will grieve not, rather find
Strength in what remains behind."
~ William Wordsworth
"Ode of Intimations of Immortality"

November 20th *Yesterday When I Was Young – Roy Clark*
"Most human beings today waste some twenty-five to thirty years of their lives before they break through the actual and conventional lies which surround them."
~ Isadora Duncan

November 21st *Everything Changes – Eartha Kitt*
"His life had seemed horrible when it was measured by its happiness, but now he seemed to gather strength as he realized that it might be measured by something else. Happiness mattered as little as pain. They came in, both of them, as all the other details of his life came in, to the elaboration of the design. He seemed for an instant to stand above the accidents of his existence, and he felt that they could not affect him again as they had done before. Whatever happened to him now would be more motive to add to the complexity of the pattern, and when the end approached he would rejoice in its completion. It would be a work of art."
~ W. Somerset Maugham
Of Human Bondage

November 22nd Here's To Life – Mary Wilson
"Life is real! Life is earnest!"
And the grave is not its goal:
Dust thou art, to dust returnest,
Was spoken not of the soul.
Not enjoyment, and not sorrow,
Is our destined end or way;
But to act, that each to-morrow
Find us farther than today…
In the world's broad field of battle,
In the bivouac of Life,
Be not like dumb, driven cattle!
Be a hero in the strife!…
Let us, then, be up and doing,
With a heart for any fate;
Still achieving, still pursuing,
Learn to labor and to wait."
    ~ Henry Wadsworth Longfellow, "A Psalm of Life"

November 23rd *Love's Been Good to Me – Nina Simone*
"I envy not in any moods
The captive void of noble rage,
The linnet born within a cage,
That never knew the summer woods:
I envy not the beast that takes
His license in the field of time,
Unfetter'd by the sense of crime,
To whom a conscience never wakes;
Nor, what may count itself as blessed,
The heart that never plighted troth

But stagnates in the weeds of sloth;
Nor any want-begotten rest.
I hold it true, whate'er befall;
I feel it, when I sorrow most;
'Tis better to have loved and lost
Than never to have loved at all."
  ~ Alfred, Lord Tennyson
  "I Envy Not in Any Moods"

November 24th *My Life's Been Grand – George Strait*
"This is the true joy of life, being used up for a purpose recognized by yourself as a mighty one; being a force of nature instead of a feverish, selfish little clot of ailments and grievances, complaining that the world will not devote itself to making you happy."
  ~ George Bernard Shaw

November 25th *Pilgrim Chapter 33 – Kris Kristofferson*
"I took the one less traveled by,
And that has made all the difference."
  ~ Robert Frost
  "The Road Not Taken"

November 26th *Good Riddance – Green Day*
"Considering that, a'l hatred driven hence,
The soul recovers radical innocence
And learns at last that it is self-delighting,
Self-appeasing, self-affrighting,
And that its own sweet will is Heaven's will;
She can, though every face should scowl

And every windy corner howl
Or every bellow burst, be happy still."
  ~ W.B. Yeats
  "A Prayer for My Daughter"

November 27th *And When I Die – Blood, Sweat & Tears*
"The tide rises, the tide falls,
The twilight darkens, the curlew calls;
Along the sea-sands damp and brown
The traveller hastens toward the town,
And the tide rises, the tide falls.
Darkness settles on roofs and walls,
But the sea, the sea in the darkness calls;
The little waves, with their soft, white hands,
Efface the footprints in the sands,
And the tides rises, the tide falls.
The morning breaks; the steeds in their stalls
Stamp and neigh, as the hostler calls;
The day returns, but nevermore
Returns the traveller to the shore,
And the tide rises, the tide falls."
  ~ Henry Wadsworth Longfellow
  "The Tide Rises, The Tide Falls"

November 28th *Precious Time - Van Morrison*
"When it's over, I want to say: all my life
I was a bride married to amazement
I was the bridegroom, taking the world into my arms.
When it is over, I don't want to wonder
if I have made of my life something particular and real.

I don't want to find myself sighing and frightened,
or full or argument.
I don't want to end up simply having visited this
world."
  ~ Mary Oliver
  "When Death Comes"

November 29th *My Way – Elvis Presley*

"Do not go gentle into that good night,
Old age should burn and rave at the close of the day;
Rage, rage against the dying of the light.
Though wise men at their end know dark is right,
Because their words had forked no lightning they
Rage, rage against the dying of the light.
Good men, the last wave by, crying how bright
Their frail deeds might have danced in a green bay,
Rage, rage against the dying of the light.
Wild men who caught and sang the sun in flight,
And learn, too late, they grieved it on its way,
Do not go gentle into that good night.
Grave men, near death, who see with blinding sight
Blind eyes could blaze like meteors and be gay,
Rage, rage against the dying of the light.
And you, my father, there on the sad height,
Curse, bless, me now with your fierce tears. I pray.
Do not go gentle into that good night.
Rage, rage against the dying of the light."
  ~ Dylan Thomas
  "Do Not Go Gentle into that Good Night"

November 30th *We'll Meet Again – Vera Lynn*

"I am not resigned to the shutting away of loving hearts in the hard ground…

The answers quick and keen, the honest look, the laughter, the love, -

They are gone. They are gone to feed the roses. Elegant and curled…

But I do not approve.

More precious was the light in your eyes than all the roses in the world.

Down, down, down into the darkness of the grave

Gently they go, the beautiful, the tender, the kind;

Quietly they go, the intelligent, the witty, the brave.

I know. But I do not approve. And I am not resigned."

~ Edna St. Vincent Millay

"Dirge Without Music"

DECEMBER: GOD

December 1ˢᵗ *Cristo È Liberazione - Pope John Paul II*
"We are summoned into the presence of God by the fact of our birth, but we become present to God only by our consent. As our faculties and capacities to relate gradually develop and unfold, the capacity to enter a relationship with God increases, and each new depth of presence requires a new consent. Each new awakening to God changes our relationship to ourselves and to everyone and everything else. Growth in faith is growth in the right perception of all reality."
~ Thomas Keating, *Intimacy with God*

December 2ⁿᵈ *Fallen Angel – Robbie Robertson*
"Looked at from the viewpoint of a Christian psychology, it was the restlessness of heart that Augustine speaks of, the generic human yearning to find (or be found by) Something utterly worthy of praise, something in which to 'rest' – not in the sense of taking one's ease, but in the sense in which a building rests on its foundation. We are foundation seekers and show by our restlessness that we are at present floating unnaturally, detached from the Solidity and Depth to which we were created to be tied. The search for the Foundation cannot, in us, be separated from the search for the understanding of our life, and so it always takes, it seems to me, the form of a search for concepts in terms of which to make sense of ourselves and our world. That is, it's always a philosophical or theological

project."
  ~ Robert C. Roberts, *God and the Philosophers*

December 3ʳᵈ *Unchained – Johnny Cash*
"By knowing God, one is released from all fetters."
  ~ *Upanishads*

December 4ᵗʰ *Anthem – Leonard Cohen*
"Nothing in himself will be perfect. Yet his very imperfections will imply some perfection which continually impregnates him and permits him thus to partake in the goodness of creation."
  ~ Rollo May, *The Springs of Creative Living*

December 5ᵗʰ *40 – U2*
"Let nothing disturb thee;
Let nothing dismay thee;
All things pass;
God never changes.
Patience attains
All that it strives for.
He who has God
Finds he lacks nothing;
God alone suffices."
  ~ St. Theresa of Jesus

December 6ᵗʰ *I've Been in the Storm – Mighty Clouds of Joy*
"True religion does not draw men out of the world but enables them to live better in it and excites their endeavors to mend it."

~ William Penn, *No Cross, No Crown*

December 7th *God Save Us All – Lenny Kravitz*
"A man content to go to heaven alone will never go to heaven."   ~ Boethius

December 8th *Brother Love's Traveling Salvation Show – Neil Diamond*
"God is said to be pleased with the soul which He finds filled with His own reality, His own love, His own truth. In a mysterious way, we please God by knowing Him, because we can only know Him by receiving His light into our hearts. Faith, then, is not only capable of penetrating the intimate substance of God's Truth, but it is an immediately redemptive knowledge of God. It 'saves' us. Its light is more than a way of speculation: it confers life. The awakening of faith not only gives light to the understanding and peace to the will: it transforms a man's moral being. He becomes a new creature. He is born again."
~ Thomas Merton, *The Ascent to Truth*

December 9th *Easy Livin' – Uriah Heap*
"Live while you live, the epicure would say,
And seize the pleasures of the present day;
Live while you live, the sacred preacher cries,
And give to God each moment as it flies.
Lord, in my view, let both united be;
I live in pleasure when I live to thee."
~ Doddridge, "Epigram on his Family Arms"

December 10th *Put Your Hand In The Hand - Ocean*

"Place your mind before the mirror of eternity! Place your soul in the brilliance of glory! Place your heart in the figure of the divine substance! And transform your whole being into the image of the Godhead Itself through contemplation!"

~ St. Clare of Assisi, *Early Documents* 44

December 11th *Day By Day - Godspell*

"There is no special designation of only certain times or kinds of activity as 'holy,' but an appreciation for the holiness of life and the goodness of creation. The spiritual aspect of existence is not experienced as something to 'add on' but is integral to and at the very heart of our lives. The Kingdom of God, in other words, is not a place but an *experience* of intensity, quality, depth, ecstasy... It is primarily a question of refining our inner and outer senses to the presence of the Holy daily in our midst... Life in this world is the life of God."

~ Thomas Ryan, *Disciplines for Christian Living*

December 12th *Love Is The Answer – England Dan & John Ford Coley*

"In love did God bring the world into existence; in love is God going to bring it to that wondrous transformed state, and in love will the world be swallowed up in the great mystery of the one who has performed all these things; in love will the whole course of the governance of creation be finally comprised." ~ St. Isaac of Syria

December 13th *Let Your Love Flow – Bellamy Brothers*
"Wouldst thou know my meaning?
Lie down in the Fire
See and taste the Flowing
Godhead through thy being;
Feel the Holy Spirit
Moving and compelling
Thee within the Flowing
Fire and Light of God."
   ~ Mechthild of Magdeburg
   The Flowing Light of the Godhead 6.29

December 14th *My Sweet Lord – George Harrison*
"We shall find we are dealing with something for which there is only one appropriate expression, '*mysterium tremendum.*' The feeling of it may at times come sweeping like a gentle tide, pervading the mind with a tranquil mood of deepest worship. It may pass over into a more set and lasting attitude of the soul, continuing, as it were, thrillingly vibrant and resonant, until at last it dies away and the soul resumes its 'profane,' non-religious mood of everyday experience. It may burst in sudden eruption from the depths of the soul with spasms and convulsions, or lead to the strangest excitements, to intoxicated frenzy, to transport, and to ecstasy... It may become the hushed, trembling, and speechless humility of the creature in the presence of – whom are what? In the presence of that which is a *mystery* inexpressible above all creatures."
   ~ Rudolf Otto, *The Idea of the Holy*

December 15th *Dweller on the Threshold – Van Morrison*
"Mystics from different religions have similar experiences. Despite all the formal variety, there are common deep structures: The goal is oneness and redemption; purification, illumination, and union are the way. Mystics of quite different religious origins often resemble, and are closer to, one another, than to the average believer in their own religion."
~ Hans Kung
Christianity and the World Religions

December 16th *Sense of Wonder – Van Morrison*
"The initiation to the lover's perspective need not be a momentous affair… It may begin simply with the shock of wonder. Suddenly. The encrustation of sophistication falls away and we find ourselves standing in front of the bare fact of being… Explanations, myths, ideologies crumble like so many sand castles. When the shock recedes, we are left with a memory of having been in the presence of the holy, the awesome and fascinating mystery… The shock of wonder is necessarily rare and intermittent. In the mystic's glimpse, as in the ecstasy of orgasm, the boundaries of individuality are melted. For a moment I see that I am a cell within the heart of Being. But like any part of an organic whole, I must rapidly fall back into my limited view and function, or else I cannot serve my purpose within the economy of the whole."
~ Sam Keen, *The Passionate Life*

December 17th *When Will I Ever Learn – Van Morrison*
"Whole, he enters the Whole. His personal self returns to its radiant, intimate, deathless source. As rivers lose name and form when they disappear into the sea, the sage leaves behind all traces when he disappears into the light. Perceiving the truth, he becomes the truth; he passes beyond all suffering, beyond death; all the knots of his heart are loosed."
~ *Third Mundaka Upanishad*

December 18th *I'll Take You There – The Staple Singers*
"There is, there can be only a single and external truth…No prophet ever reveals it for the first time, no seer discovers it. All only rediscover it. It never changes or evolves; only its form of presentation does that. But before it can manifest in our world, it must find human minds sufficiently prepared to be able to receive it and sufficiently developed to be able to comprehend and teach it."
~ Paul Brunton, *The Spiritual Crisis of Man*

December 19th *I Go To The Rock – Whitney Houston*
"To return to the source is a familiar journey for the religious person. In all of life's experiences, those smooth and those rocky, the religious person seeks funding and direction from the deepest ground of personal existence. This habit of returning to the source is neither an escape nor a solution… [The religious person] repairs there to consult larger purposes and reaffirm enduring values in order to act more

creatively in the immediate frays of personal and interpersonal existence."

~ John Shea, *The Challenge of Jesus*

December 20th *Testify – Sounds of Blackness*
"But whether we stay in the tradition of our parents, or travel away and back again, or travel away and find God calling us to another tradition, the graced possibility is that each historically valid tradition has a core of truth that reaches toward the single, loving, energetic Source of creation. This core is often covered over with distortions and superficial trappings, and it may be buried under claims of exclusivity, but I believe it exists, deeply and very alive, within all major spiritual traditions. It can be found beneath Anglican formality, Roman authority, and Quaker simplicity; behind Methodist fellowship, Presbyterian morality, and Baptist freedom. It lies in the depths of Evangelical and Pentecostal zeal. It forms the matrix that binds Jews together with each other and with the Lord. It infuses the poignant devotion of Bhakti Yoga and the discriminating insight of Theravada Buddhism. It is the background upon which are painted the vibrant colors of Tantra. It is at the center of the Sufi's twirl and the Navaho's dance. It is the correct answer to every Zen koan."

~ Gerald G. May, Will & Spirit

December 21st *We Give You Thanks – Sounds of Blackness*
"I thank you, my Creator and Lord, that you have given

me these joys in your creation, this ecstasy over the works of your hands. I have made known the glory of your works to men as far as my finite spirit was able to comprehend your infinity. If I have said anything wholly unworthy of you, or have aspired after my own glory, graciously forgive me."

~ Johannes Kepler, "Prayer for Our Creator God"

December 22nd *Man of God – Neil Diamond*

"Reunited in this principle with the rest of the universe, he does not join any of the sects which all contradict one another. His religion is the most ancient and the most widespread; for the simple worship of God preceded all of the systems of the world…He has brothers from Peking to Cayenne, and he counts all the sages for his fellows. He believes that religion exists neither in the opinions of an unintelligible metaphysics, nor in vain shows, but in worship and in justice. To do good is his worship, to submit to God is his creed."

~ Voltaire, "Theist;" *Dictionary*

December 23rd *How Great Thou Art – Elvis Presley*

"And how much weight has all erroneous talk about God's nature and works (although there never has been nor can be any such talk that is not erroneous) compared with the one truth that all men who have addressed God really meant him? For whoever pronounces the word God and really means Thou, addresses, no matter what his delusion, the true Thou of his life that cannot be restricted by any other and to whom he stands in a relationship that includes all others."

~ Martin Buber, *I and Thou*

December 24ᵗʰ *O Holy Night - Celine Dion*

"Faith is deeper, richer, more personal. It is engendered and sustained by a religious tradition, in some cases and to some degree by its doctrines; but it is a quality of the person, not of the system. It is an orientation of the personality, to oneself, to one's neighbor, to the universe; a total response; a way of seeing whatever one sees and of handling whatever one handles; a capacity to live at a more than mundane level; to see, to feel, to act in terms of a transcendent dimension. Belief, on the other hand, is the holding of certain ideas. Some might see it as the intellect's translation of transcendence into ostensible terms."

~ Wilfred Cantrell Smith, *Faith & Belief*

December 25ᵗʰ *Joy To The World – Aretha Franklin*

"If an Emerson were forced to be a Wesley, or a Moody forced to be a Whitman, the total human consciousness of the divine would suffer. The divine can mean no single quality, it must mean a group of qualities, by being champions of which in alternation, different men may all find worthy missions. Each attitude being a syllable in human nature's total message, it takes the whole of us to spell the meaning out completely."

~ William James, *The Varieties of Religious Experience*

December 26th *How Can I Keep from Singing - Eva Cassidy*
"I have felt
A presence that disturbs me with the joy
Of elevated thoughts; a sense sublime
Of something far more deeply interfused,
Whose dwelling is the light of setting suns,
And the round ocean and the living air,
And the blue sky, and in the mind of man:
A motion and a spirit, that impels
All thinking things, all objects of thought,
And rolls through all things."
 ~ William Wordsworth, "Tintern Abbey"

December 27th *Deep Peace - Donovan*
"The Kingdom of Heaven is not a place, but a state of mind."
 ~ John Burroughs, *The Light of Day*

December 28th *The Evernow – Donovan*
"Eternal life is not continuation of life after death. Eternal life is beyond past, present, and future: we come from it, we live in its presence, we return to it. It is never absent – it is the divine life in which we are rooted."
 ~ Paul Tillich, *The Eternal Now*

December 29th *Be Not Afraid – Daniel O'Donnell*
"No coward soul is mine,
No trembler in the world's storm-troubled sphere:
I see Heaven's glories shine,

And faith shines equal, arming me from fear.
O God within my breast,
Almighty, ever-present Deity!
Life--that in me has rest,
As I--undying Life--have power in thee!
Vain are the thousand creeds
That move men's hearts: unutterably vain;
Worthless as withered weeds,
Or idlest froth amid the boundless main,
To waken doubt in one
Holding so fast by thine infinity;
So surely anchored on
The stedfast rock of immortality.
With wide-embracing love
Thy spirit animates eternal years,
Pervades and broods above,
Changes, sustains, dissolves, creates, and rears.
Though earth and man were gone,
And suns and universes ceased to be,
And Thou were left alone,
Every existence would exist in Thee.
There is not room for Death,
Nor atom that his might could render void:
Thou--THOU art Being and Breath,
And what THOU art may never be destroyed."
   ~ Emily Bronte, "No Coward Soul Is Mine"

December 30th *Up To The Mountain – Solomon Burke*
"Friend, hope for the Guest while you are alive.
Jump into experience while you are alive!

Think...and think... while you are alive.
If you don't break your ropes while you're alive,
do you think
ghosts will do it after?
The idea that the soul will join with the ecstatic
just because the body is rotten-
that is all fantasy.
What is found now is found then.
If you find nothing now,
you will simply end up with an apartment in the City
of Death.
If you make love with the divine now, in the next life
 you will have the face of satisfied desire.
So plunge into the truth, find out who the Teacher is,
Believe in the Great Sound!
Kabir says this: When the Guest is being searched for,
it is the intensity of the longing for the Guest that
does all the work.
Look at me, and you will see a slave of that intensity."
  ~ Kabir, "Friend, Hope for the Guest"

December 31st *Beautiful Vision – Van Morrison*
"Men's curiosity searches past and future
And clings to that dimension. But to apprehend
The point of intersection of the timeless
With time, is an occupation for the saint –
No occupation either, but something given
And taken, in a lifetime's death in love,
Ardor and selflessness and self-surrender.
For most of us, there is only the unintended

Moment, the moment in and out of time.
The distraction fit, lost in a shaft of sunlight,
The wild thyme unseen, or the winter lightening,
Or the waterfall, or music heard so deeply
That it is not heard at all, but you are the music
While the music lasts. These are only hints and guesses,
Hints followed by guesses, and the rest
Is prayer, observance, discipline, thought and action.
The hint half-guessed, the gift half understood is
Incarnation.
Here the impossible Union
Of spheres of existence is actual,
Here the past and future
Are conquered and reconciled,
Where action were otherwise movement
Of that which is only moved
And has in it no source of movement –
Driven by daemonic, chthonic
Powers. And right action is freedom
From past and future also
Never here to be realized;
Who are only undefeated
Because we have gone on trying;
We, content at last
If our temporal reversion nourish
(Not too far from the yew tree)
The life of significant soil."
  ~ T.S. Eliot, "Dry Salvages"

ABOUT THE AUTHOR

After becoming a wee mystic at age four, the author went on to live a life of loving devotion, heart-breaking estrangement, passionate searching, and honest thinking on her way to better understanding God and better understanding what she does not understand about God. Along the way, she also earned a B.A. in Psychology with minors in Philosophy, Sociology, and Political Science and a M.A. in Counseling. She is the author of GOD-centric and GOD-centric Interior Spiritual Disciplines and the Oz behind the Life of Significant Soil and Liberal Devotional web sites. If she conjures up enough will, she may begin blogging as Freelance Monkette.

www.ingramcontent.com/pod-product-compliance
Lightning Source LLC
Chambersburg PA
CBHW070356290526
45790CB00004B/1511